SPECTRUM

1B

A Communicative Course in English

Diane Warshawsky
with *Donald R. H. Byrd*

Donald R. H. Byrd *Project Director*

Anna Veltfort *Art Director*

Regents/Prentice Hall
Englewood Cliffs, NJ 07632

Library of Congress has cataloged the full edition of this title as follows:

Warshawsky, Diane.
    Spectrum 1, a communicative course in English / Diane Warshawsky
with Donald R.H. Byrd; Donald R. H. Byrd, project director; Anna
Veltfort, art director.
        p   cm.
Also published in a two book split edition
ISBN 0-13-829862-9
    1. English language--Textbooks for foreign speakers.   I. Byrd,
Donald R.H.   II. Title.
PE1128.W36 1992
428.2'4--dc20   91- 40867
                                                                        CIP

ISBN (1A) 0-13-829870-X   ISBN (1B) 0-13-829888-2

Editorial Project Director: Mary Vaughn

Development Editor: Deborah Brennan
Senior Editor: Larry Anger
Audio Editor: Stephanie Karras

Production Editor: Shari Toron
Pre-Press Buyer: Ray Keating
Manufacturing Buyer: Lori Bulwin
Scheduler: Leslie Coward
Technical Support and Assistance: David Riccardi

Cover Design: Roberto de Vicq
Interior Concept and Page-by-Page Design: Anna Veltfort
Audio Program Production: Phyllis Dolgin

Publisher: Tina B. Carver

 © 1992 by Prentice Hall, Inc.
A Simon & Schuster Company
Englewood Cliffs, NJ 07632

Printed in the United States of America

10 9 8 7 6 5 4 3 2

ISBN 0-13-829888-2

Prentice Hall International (UK) Limited, *London*
Prentice Hall of Australia Pty. Limited, *Sydney*
Prentice Hall Canada, Inc., *Toronto*
Prentice Hall Hispanoamericana, S.A., *Mexico*
Prentice Hall of India Private Limited, *New Delhi*
Prentice Hall of Japan, Inc., *Tokyo*
Simon & Schuster Asia Pte. Ltd, *Singapore*
Editora Prentice Hall do Brasil, Ltda., *Rio de Janeiro*

INTRODUCTION

Spectrum 1A and 1B represent the first level of a six-level course designed for adolescent and adult learners of English. The student book, workbook, and audio program for each level provide practice in all four communication skills, with a special focus on listening and speaking. Levels 1 and 2 are appropriate for beginning students and "false" beginners. Levels 3 and 4 are intended for intermediate classes, and 5 and 6 for advanced learners of English. The first four levels are offered in split editions — 1A, 1B, 2A, 2B, 3A, 3B, 4A, and 4B. The student books and workbooks for levels 1 to 4 are also available in full editions.

Spectrum is a "communicative" course in English, based on the idea that communication is not merely an end-product of language study, but rather the very process through which a new language is acquired. *Spectrum* involves students in this process from the very beginning by providing them with useful, natural English along with opportunities to discuss topics of personal interest and to communicate their own thoughts, feelings, and ideas.

In *Spectrum*, understanding a new language is considered the starting point for communication. The student books thus emphasize the importance of comprehension, both as a useful skill and as a natural means of acquiring a language. Students begin each unit by listening to and reading conversations that provide rich input for language learning. Accompanying activities enhance comprehension and give students time to absorb new vocabulary and structures. Throughout the unit students encounter readings and dialogues containing structures and expressions not formally introduced until later units or levels. The goal is to provide students with a continuous stream of input that challenges their current knowledge of English, thereby allowing them to progress naturally to a higher level of competence.

Spectrum emphasizes interaction as another vital step in language acquisition. Interaction begins with simple communication tasks that motivate students to use the same structure a number of times as they exchange real information about themselves and other topics. This focused practice builds confidence and fluency and prepares students for more open-ended activities involving role playing, discussion, and problem solving. These activities give students control of the interaction and enable them to develop strategies for expressing themselves and negotiating meaning in an English-speaking environment.

The *Spectrum* syllabus is organized around functions and structures practiced in thematic lessons. Both functions and structures are carefully graded according to simplicity and usefulness. Structures are presented in clear paradigms with informative usage notes. Thematic lessons provide interesting topics for interaction and a meaningful vehicle for introducing vocabulary.

Student Book 1B consists of seven units, each divided into one- and two-page lessons. The first lesson in each unit presents a series of authentic conversations, providing input for comprehension and language acquisition. A preview activity prepares students to understand the cultural material in the conversations. New functions and structures are then practiced through interactive tasks in several thematic lessons. A two-page, fully illustrated comprehension lesson provides further input in the form of a dialogue, pronunciation activity, and listening exercise all related to the storyline for the level. This lesson includes a role-playing activity as well. The final lesson of the unit presents authentic documents such as advertisements and news articles for reading comprehension practice. Review lessons follow units 1 to 4 and units 5 to 7.

Workbook 1B is carefully coordinated with the student book. Workbook lessons provide listening and writing practice on the functions, structures, and vocabulary introduced in the corresponding student book lessons. Units end with a guided composition related to the theme of the reading in the student book.

Audio Program 1B offers two cassettes for the student book with all conversations, model dialogues, listening activities, and readings dramatized by professional actors in realistic recordings with music and sound effects. A third cassette includes the workbook listening activities.

Teacher's Edition 1B features full-sized reproductions of each student-book page with teaching suggestions, listening scripts, and answer keys on the facing page. Listening scripts and answer keys for the workbook appear in the appendix.

A **Testing Package** includes a placement test as well as midterm and final tests for each level.

UNIT	PAGES	THEMES	FUNCTIONS
1 **Lessons 1 – 7**	B1–10	Clothing and personal belongings Colors	Talk about clothing and personal belongings Compliment someone Look for a lost item Ask where something is Give directions Talk about the past
2 **Lessons 8 – 14**	B11–22	Suggestions Objections Time	Talk about what people are doing Talk about the weather Make a suggestion Object or agree Ask what time it is Find out hours Talk about movies Talk about likes and dislikes Talk about feelings
3 **Lessons 15 – 19**	B23–32	Foods Shopping	Talk about favorite foods Shop for food Ask about prices Ask for something you want Make a shopping list
4 **Lessons 20 – 25**	B33–42	Past activities	Talk about past activities Ask about the weekend Ask about the past Talk about the past
Review of units 1 – 4	B43–46	Review	Review

S E Q U E N C E

LANGUAGE	FORMS	SKILLS

What color are her gloves?
That's a nice blouse.
They're on the table.
I don't have my keys!
Is there a telephone near here?
    There's one upstairs.
Where were you?
	Colors
	Demonstrative pronouns: *that*
	    and *those*
	In, *on*, *under*, and *behind*
	Possessive adjectives
	There is
	The past of *be*
		Listen to descriptions of clothing
		    and personal belongings
		Listen to the intonation of
		    information questions
		Read a short newspaper article
		Write an opinion about TV (WB)

He's reading a book. It's hot and sunny. Let's go to a museum. That's a good idea. / That's too boring. What time is it? What time do you open? What's playing this week? I don't really like old movies. I'm having a wonderful time.	The present continuous *Let's . . .* Weather Articles: *a*, *an*, and *the* Time Subject questions Placement of adjectives	Listen to a weather report Listen to suggestions and objections Listen for times Read a page from a tour guide Write a movie review (WB)
Steak is my favorite food. I'll take these bananas. How much are oranges? I'd like some pears, please. Do you need any onions? We need two pounds of chicken.	Foods Demonstrative adjectives: *this*, *that*, *these*, and *those* *How much* *Some* and *any*	Listen to an article about foods Listen to a radio ad Read a short magazine article Write a note (WB)

They visited their friends.
They went to the ballet.
How was your weekend?
What did you do?
She went to the office.
She was at the office.
She was in the office.
	The past tense
	Information questions in the
	    past tense
	To, *at*, and *in* with the definite
	    article
		Listen for information about
		    people's past activities
		Listen to the pronunciation of
		    irregular past tense verbs
		Read a short magazine article
		Write a letter to a friend (WB)

Review	Review	Review

LANGUAGE	FORMS	SKILLS
Nice day. I live in the city. There's always something to do. In my opinion, it's the only place to live. I love nightclubs. But the nightclubs here are awful. New York is my favorite city. Robert likes classical music, and I do too. Robert doesn't like mystery novels, and I don't either.	*There is* and *there are* Nouns with and without *the* Rejoinders: *too* and *either*	Listen to small talk Listen to opinions Read a questionnaire Write about your favorite city (WB)
Could you open the window? Could you answer it for me? What do you do? What are you doing? I'm doing just great. How's Betsy doing? Say hi to her for me. I've got two tickets for the baseball game. Do you want to go? Would you like to join us? I'd like to, but I can't. I have to work on Saturday. When is it? In December. / On Sunday. / At five o'clock.	*Could you . . . ?* Pronouns as objects of prepositions Simple present vs. present continuous *Have got* *Have to* and *have got to* Prepositions *in*, *on*, and *at*	Listen to requests Listen to invitations Read a short magazine article Write an invitation (WB)
Is this your hammer or mine? A plumber's job is hard work, but the pay is good. Where can you get some aspirin? There's a drugstore on Ridge Road. Can I get you anything? I'm like Manolo. I always have a big lunch around 2:00 P.M.	Possessive pronouns Conjunction *but* Impersonal pronoun *you* Frequency adverbs	Listen to opinions about jobs Listen to someone ordering in a coffee shop Read a short magazine article Write a postcard (WB)
Review	Review	Review

PREVIEW

FUNCTIONS/THEMES	LANGUAGE	FORMS
Clothing and personal belongings	What color are her gloves?	Colors
Compliment someone	That's a nice blouse.	Demonstrative pronouns (*that*, *those*)
Look for a lost item	They're on the table. I don't have my keys!	*In, on, under,* and *behind* Possessive adjectives
Ask where something is Give directions	Is there a telephone near here? There's one upstairs.	*There is*
Talk about the past	Where were you?	The past of *be*

Preview the conversations.

What's Amanda's problem? What do you think she does?

The man above is giving a friend a compliment. Do you compliment your friends? When?

1. Lost and Found

Amanda Kelly goes to the hospital to see her doctor.

A

Nurse Here you are, Mrs. Kelly. Your next appointment with Dr. Wood is on Tuesday, April 6th, at ten o'clock.
Mrs. Kelly Thank you.
Nurse By the way, that's a nice dress. You look good in green.
Mrs. Kelly Oh, thank you. It's my favorite color. Uh . . . is there a pay phone on this floor?
Nurse Yes, there's one next to the elevators.
Mrs. Kelly Which way are the elevators?
Nurse Down the hall on the right. Just follow the blue line.
Mrs. Kelly Thank you.
Nurse Good-bye, Mrs. Kelly. See you next month.
Mrs. Kelly Bye.

B

Woman Excuse me, I found this wallet on the floor over there.
Nurse Oh, thank you. I'll take it to the Lost and Found.

Mr. Kelly Amanda! There you are. It's after six. Where were you? I was worried.
Mrs. Kelly I was at the doctor's office, remember?
Mr. Kelly Oh, that's right. Is everything O.K.?
Mrs. Kelly Yes, everything's fine. How was your day?
Mr. Kelly Not bad.

Mrs. Kelly Oh, no!
Mr. Kelly What's wrong?
Mrs. Kelly I don't have my wallet!

Clerk Lost and Found. May I help you?
Mrs. Kelly Yes, this is Amanda Kelly. I lost my wallet this afternoon. Do you have it by any chance?
Clerk Let's see. . . . What color is it?
Mrs. Kelly Red.
Clerk Just one moment, please. . . . Yes, it's here, Mrs. Kelly.
Mrs. Kelly Oh, what a relief! (*to husband*) He has it there.

LOST AND FOUND

Figure it out

1. Listen to the conversations. Say *true* or *false*.

1. Mrs. Kelly's wallet is blue. *False*
2. Mrs. Kelly's favorite color is green.
3. Mrs. Kelly lost her wallet in the elevator.
4. Mrs. Kelly's husband was worried.

2. Listen again. Match.

1. You look good in green.
2. Is there a pay phone on this floor?
3. Which way are the elevators?
4. How was your day?
5. What color is it?

a. Red.
b. There's one next to the elevators.
c. Oh, thank you.
d. Down the hall on the right.
e. Not bad.

2. That's a nice dress!

CLOTHING AND PERSONAL BELONGINGS • COLORS

1 ► Look at the picture. Match the questions and answers.
► Listen to check your work.

1. What color is Angela's dress?
2. What color are her gloves?
3. What color is Michael's suit?
4. What color are his shoes?

a. They're black.
b. It's blue.
c. They're brown.
d. It's gray.

Angela**'s** dress	➜ **her** dress
Michael**'s** suit	➜ **his** suit

2 ► Ask and answer questions about the people in the picture.

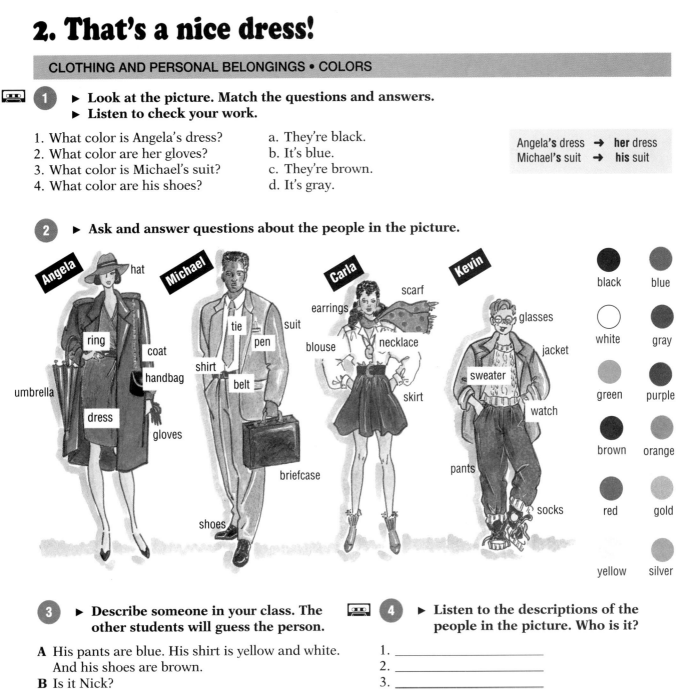

3 ► Describe someone in your class. The other students will guess the person.

A His pants are blue. His shirt is yellow and white. And his shoes are brown.
B Is it Nick?
A Yes, it is. (No, it isn't. It's John.)

4 ► Listen to the descriptions of the people in the picture. Who is it?

1. _____
2. _____
3. _____
4. _____

COMPLIMENT SOMEONE

5 ► The four people above are talking. Listen and complete their conversations.

1. **Kevin** That's a nice _____ . You look good in _____ .
   Angela Thank you.

2. **Michael** Those are beautiful _____ .
   Carla Thanks. They were a gift.

Singular	Plural
That's a nice hat.	**Those are** nice gloves.
It was a gift.	**They were** a gift.

► Compliment each of your classmates on a personal belonging or item of clothing.

3. I lost my keys!

LOOK FOR A LOST ITEM • *IN, ON, UNDER,* AND *BEHIND*

1 ▶ **Complete the conversation with the expressions in the picture.**
  ▶ **Listen to check your answers.**
  ▶ **Act out the conversation with a partner.**

A Hurry! We're late!
B Wait. I don't have my keys.
A They're right there _____ .
B You're right. But where's my wallet?

A Is that it _____ ?
B Yes. Thanks. Now I just need my coat and hat.
A Look. Your hat is _____ .
B Great! And here's my coat . . . _____ .

in the closet

on the coffee table

under the desk

behind the sofa

2 ▶ **Listen to the conversation below.**
  ▶ **Practice similar conversations using the information in the pictures.**

A Oh, no!
B What's wrong?
A I lost my gloves.
B They're over there on the table.
A Oh, what a relief!

gloves on the table

shoes behind the door

keys in my pocket

glasses on the desk

credit card under the sofa

LOOK FOR A LOST ITEM • POSSESSIVE ADJECTIVES

3 ▶ **Study the frame.**

Possessive adjectives			
I You He She We They	lost	my your his her our their	gloves.

4 ▶ **Fill in the blanks with the correct possessive adjectives.**

I lost _____ glasses.

My wife and I lost _____ traveler's checks.

My daughter lost _____ umbrella.

These people lost _____ passports.

Here's _____ wallet, sir.

4. Locations in a building

ASK WHERE SOMETHING IS • GIVE DIRECTIONS

1 ▶ **Answer the questions using the pictures below.**
▶ **Listen to check your answers.**

1. Is there a telephone near here? *Yes. There's one upstairs.*
2. Excuse me. Where's the drinking fountain? *It's down the hall on the left.*
3. Excuse me. Which way are the restrooms?
4. Is there a cafeteria here?
5. Which way is the exit?
6. Excuse me. Which way are the elevators?

> **Is there** a cafeteria here?
> Yes, **there's one** downstairs.
> No, **there isn't**.

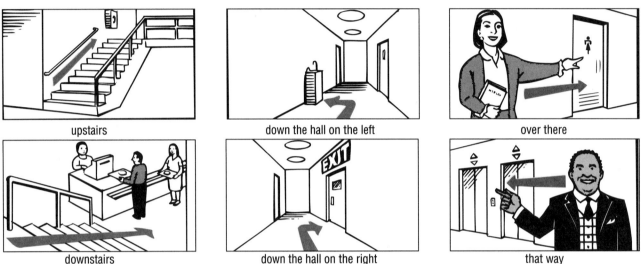

upstairs	down the hall on the left	over there
downstairs	down the hall on the right	that way

2 ▶ **Ask and answer questions about the places in the floor plan below.**

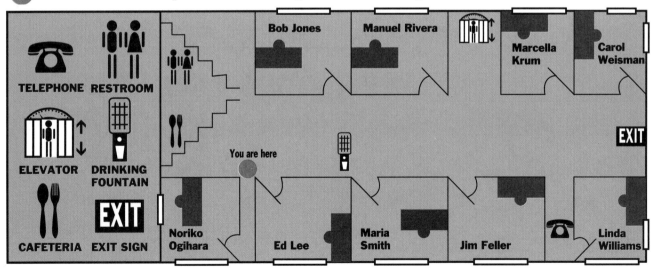

TELEPHONE   RESTROOM
ELEVATOR   DRINKING FOUNTAIN
CAFETERIA   EXIT SIGN

Bob Jones   Manuel Rivera   Marcella Krum   Carol Weisman

You are here

EXIT

Noriko Ogihara   Ed Lee   Maria Smith   Jim Feller   Linda Williams

3 ▶ **Talk with your classmates.**

Ask where places are in your school building. Use the questions in the box or your own questions.

> Where are the restrooms?
> Is there a drinking fountain on this floor?
> Which way is the exit?
> Is there a cafeteria near here?

5. Where were you?

1 ▶ **Study the frames: The Past of *Be***

Information questions		
	was	he? she? your wallet?
Where	**were**	you? they?

Affirmative statements		
He She It I	**was**	
		at work.
We They	**were**	

Negative statements		
He She It I	**wasn't** **(was not)**	
		at school.
We They	**weren't** **(were not)**	

2 ▶ **Complete the conversations with the past tense of *be*.**
▶ **Listen to check your answers.**
▶ **Act out the conversations with a partner.**

1. **A** Where ___were___ you yesterday?
   B I _____ sick. How _____ class?
   A It _____ interesting.
   B I'm sorry I _____ (not) here.

2. **A** I found my glasses.
   B Where _____ they?
   A They _____ in my car.
   B I'm glad you found them.

3. **A** You _____ (not) at work on Monday. Where _____ you?
   B We _____ at home.
   A Oh? What _____ wrong?
   B Our son _____ sick.

3 ▶ **Listen to the conversation below.**
▶ **Act out the conversations the teacher has with each student in the picture.**

Teacher Susan, you're late. Where were you?
Susan I was in the restroom.

6. Tryout

Carolyn Duval is trying out for a part in a television commercial.

1

Carolyn Good morning, my name's Carolyn Duval. I have a ten o'clock appointment with Mr. Anderson.

Mr. Anderson Yes, hello, Ms. Duval. I'm Jack Anderson. It's nice to meet you. This is my assistant Vicky Wu.

Vicky Wu Here's the script. Take a minute or two to read it over. That's Bob Velez over there. He's also trying out for this commercial.

2

Husband (*Holds up shirt*) Honey, this isn't my shirt.

Wife Yes, it is.

Husband But my shirts aren't this white.

Wife They weren't before, but they are now — now that we use *All-Bright*. (*Holds up box*)

Husband *All-Bright*? What's that?

Wife A new detergent — it gets all our laundry clean and bright. I was lost until I found *All-Bright*. What a wonderful detergent!

Husband (*Kisses wife*) What a wonderful wife!

3. Figure it out

True or *false*?

1. Carolyn Duval has a ten o'clock appointment at the doctor's office. *False.*
2. Carolyn Duval and Bob Velez are married.
3. Carolyn wants a part in a television commercial.
4. *All-Bright* is a detergent for washing clothes.

Thank you very much, Ms. Duval. We'll call you in a few days.

O.K. Thanks for your time, Mr. Anderson.

4. Listen in

Carolyn needs to make a phone call. Read the statements below. Then listen to the conversation and say *true* or *false*.

1. The phone is in the lobby next to the coffee shop.
2. The lobby is on the second floor.

5. Your turn

Carolyn lost her umbrella at the tryout. Complete the conversation below. Then act it out with a partner.

Carolyn _____
  Vicky What's wrong?
Carolyn _____
  Vicky What color is it?
Carolyn _____
  Vicky I think it's over there
         in the corner.
Carolyn _____

6. How to say it

Practice this conversation.

A Oh, no!

B What's wrong?

A I lost my wallet!

B Is this it?

A Yes! What a relief!

7. Listen in

Carolyn got the part. Two months later, George and Loretta are watching TV with Nick and Stella, and they see Carolyn's commercial. Read the conversation below. Then listen to the conversation and fill in the missing words.

George Hey, look! It's _____ .
Loretta You're _____ ! What a surprise!
  Stella Carolyn Duval . . . who's that?
Loretta She _____ next door. She's an _____ .
   Nick She's really _____ .
Loretta Shh!

7. Do People Watch Too Much TV?

Koji Kawabe

I know a lot of parents are worried because their children watch TV all the time. In fact, I read somewhere that the average child in the United States watches 19,000 hours of TV by the time he or she finishes high school. And that truly is a lot. But personally, I don't think TV is so bad. There are a lot of interesting programs on TV and you can learn a lot about the world. It's a great invention.

Rosa Hernandez

The real problem is the commercials. They stop every ten minutes to show a commercial. When I get home at night, I want to relax and enjoy myself. I'm not interested in watching ads for perfume and laundry detergent and breakfast cereal. I certainly don't think I'll be a better person or more beautiful or healthy if I buy those things.

William Owen

I like to watch TV, but I think people spend too much time in front of their TV sets. There are a lot of dumb programs on TV. Also, the television is not a very social machine. People should do things together—spend time with friends, play sports, go to plays and concerts, things like that.

Cheryl Brady

Definitely. We all watch too much. TV influences and changes our lives — not always for the better. For example, many experts feel that violent TV programs make children more aggressive—they fight or interrupt other children who are playing calmly—and that they will grow up to be aggressive adults.

1. **Read the survey. Who doesn't answer the question?**

2. **What's your opinion? Do people watch too much television?**

PREVIEW

FUNCTIONS/THEMES	LANGUAGE	FORMS
Talk about what people are doing	He's reading a book.	The present continuous
Talk about the weather	It's hot and sunny.	Weather
Make a suggestion Object or agree Ask what time it is Find out hours	Let's go to a museum. That's a good idea./That's too boring. What time is it? What time do you open?	*Let's* . . . Articles: *a*, *an*, and *the* Time
Talk about movies Talk about likes and dislikes Talk about feelings	What's playing this week? I don't really like old movies. I'm having a wonderful time.	Subject questions Placement of adjectives

Preview the conversations.

French influence is very strong in New Orleans, especially in the French Quarter. There are many good French restaurants there.

There is also a Spanish influence in the city, particularly in the architecture.

African-Americans in New Orleans developed jazz in the late 1800s. It is now popular all over the world.

Discuss these questions with the class.

1. Where's New Orleans?
2. Think of things that New Orleans is famous for.
3. What kind of things can you do in New Orleans?

8. Any suggestions?

 Patty and Paul Sasa are spending their honeymoon in New Orleans.

A

Patty What a beautiful day! Are you having a good time?
Paul Yeah, I'm having a wonderful time.
Patty I am too. I just love New Orleans!
Paul I do too!

B

Patty Paul . . . What are you doing?
Paul I'm calling my mother. *(Dialing phone)*
Mrs. Sasa Hello?
Paul Hi, Mom. It's Paul.
Mrs. Sasa Paul! How's New Orleans?
Paul Great! We're sightseeing and going to museums.
Mrs. Sasa How's the weather?
Paul Oh, it's sunny and beautiful.
Mrs. Sasa Lucky you. It's cold here, and it's snowing.

C

Patty Uh-oh. . .
Paul What's wrong?
Patty Uh . . . I think it's . . . raining!
Paul Come on! Let's run.

D

Paul What do you want to do? Any suggestions?
Patty Let's go to a movie. *Love on a Rainy Afternoon* is playing near the hotel.
Paul But we go to the movies all the time at home.
Patty O.K., then, let's go to a museum.
Paul Good idea. Oh, wait—what time is it?
Patty It's a quarter after five.
Paul Too late. The museums close at five.
Patty Oh, right. They're open from ten to five.

E

Paul I'm hungry.

Patty Me too. Let's go out to dinner.

Paul O.K. What do you want to eat?

Patty How about oysters? New Orleans is famous for its oysters.

Paul You know I don't like oysters.

Patty Well, how about a French restaurant?

Paul No. That's too expensive.

Patty Well, where *do* you want to go?

F

Patty I'm exhausted. Let's go back to the hotel.

Paul It's too early. It's only twenty to ten! Let's go to a jazz club. Now let's see . . . who's playing?

Patty Oh, honey . . . I'm too tired.

Paul Oh, look! Toots Bixler is playing at the Savoy. The show starts at ten o'clock. Come on! Let's go!

Figure it out

1. Listen to the conversations. Say *true*, *false*, or *it doesn't say*.

1. Patty and Paul don't like New Orleans. *False.*
2. Patty calls her mother from New Orleans.
3. Patty likes oysters.
4. Paul likes French food.
5. Patty and Paul go to a French restaurant.
6. At twenty to ten, Paul wants to go back to the hotel.

2. Listen again and choose the best response to each sentence.

1. I just love New Orleans!
   (a.) I do too.
   b. I am too.

2. How's the weather?
   a. That's good.
   b. It's beautiful.

3. Any suggestions?
   a. Let's go to a movie.
   b. We're sightseeing.

4. Let's go to a museum.
   a. Me too.
   b. That's a good idea.

5. What time is it?
   a. It's a quarter after five.
   b. It's sunny.

6. What are you doing?
   a. I'm calling my mother.
   b. Let's go back to the hotel.

7. Who's playing?
   a. *Love on a Rainy Afternoon*.
   b. Toots Bixler.

9. What are you doing?

 1 ▶ **Study the picture and complete the sentences.**
▶ **Listen to check your answers.**

1. _Boris_ is dancing.
2. _____ is drinking wine.
3. _____ is going to a movie.

4. _____ are talking in the street.
5. _____ is playing jazz.
6. _____ are eating oysters.

2 ▶ **Study the frames: The Present Continuous**

Information questions			Statements				
	are	you	I	**'m**			
		they	We They	**'re**	(not)	eating.	
What							
	is	he	He She	**'s**			
		she					
			It	**'s**		raining.	

Yes-no questions			Short answers		
Are	you		Yes,	I	**am.**
	they		No,		**'m not.**
		listening?	Yes,	we	**are.**
Is	he		No,	they	**aren't.**
	she		Yes,	he	**is.**
			No,	she	**isn't.**
Is	it	**raining?**	Yes,	it	**is.**
			No,		**isn't.**

do + **ing** → doing
have + **ing** → having
run + **ing** → running

 3 ▶ **Listen to the conversation below.**
▶ **Have a similar conversation about the people in the picture.**

A What's Boris doing?
B He's dancing.
A Is he having a good time?
B Yes, he is.

4 ▶ **Talk with your classmates.**

What are you doing? What about your family and friends? Where are they right now? What are they doing?

My father is at work right now. He's probably talking on the telephone.

10. How's the weather?

1 ▶ Read the weather map and circle *a* or *b*.
▶ Listen to check your answers.

1. In Reykjavik, it's . . .
   a. very cold and snowing.
   b. very cold and raining.

2. In Dublin, it's . . .
   a. cool and snowing.
   b. cool and raining.

3. In Prague, it's . . .
   a. sunny and warm.
   b. cloudy and cool.

4. In Lisbon, it's . . .
   a. warm and raining.
   b. cloudy and cool.

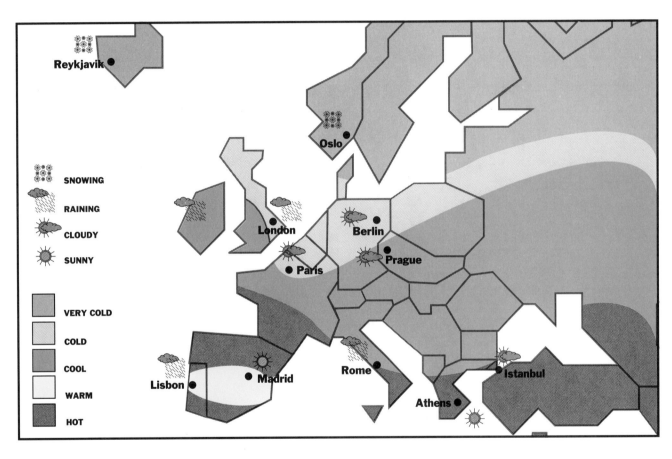

It's cold. It's cool. It's warm. It's hot.

2 ▶ Ask and answer questions about the map.

A How's the weather in Dublin?
B It's raining.

3 ▶ Talk with your classmates. How's the weather in your country right now?

11. Let's go to the beach.

1 ▶ **Match the woman's suggestions below with her husband's objections.**
▶ **Listen to check your answers.**

Let's go out to dinner.
Let's go dancing.
Let's go for a walk in the park.
Let's go to the beach.
Let's stay home and watch TV.

I'm too tired. It's too cold.
That's too boring. That's too dangerous.
That's too expensive.

2 ▶ **Listen to the two possible conversations.**
▶ **Act out the conversations with a partner.**

A What do you want to do? Any suggestions?

B Let's go to a movie.

Let's + verb ➔ Let's go out to dinner.

A That's a good idea.   **A** That's too boring. Let's go dancing instead.

3 ▶ **Study the frame.**

Articles: *a* (*an*) and *the*

Let's go to **a** museum.
O.K. How about **the** art museum on Rampart Street?

4 ▶ **Complete the conversation with *a* (*an*) or *the*.**
▶ **Listen to check your answers.**

A Let's go to _____ museum.
B O.K. How about _____ Voodoo Museum on Dumaine Street?
A No, I was there yesterday. Let's go to _____ art museum instead.
B No. I don't think that _____ art museum here is very interesting.

ASK WHAT TIME IT IS • TIME

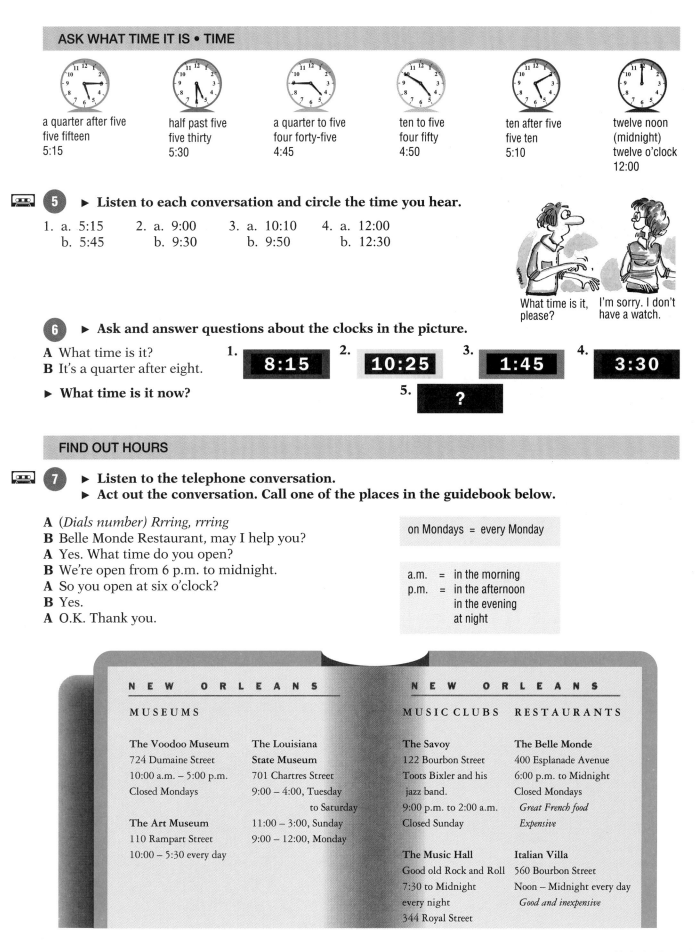

a quarter after five
five fifteen
5:15

half past five
five thirty
5:30

a quarter to five
four forty-five
4:45

ten to five
four fifty
4:50

ten after five
five ten
5:10

twelve noon
(midnight)
twelve o'clock
12:00

5 ► Listen to each conversation and circle the time you hear.

1. a. 5:15
   b. 5:45
2. a. 9:00
   b. 9:30
3. a. 10:10
   b. 9:50
4. a. 12:00
   b. 12:30

What time is it, please?   I'm sorry. I don't have a watch.

6 ► Ask and answer questions about the clocks in the picture.

A What time is it?
B It's a quarter after eight.

1. **8:15** 2. **10:25** 3. **1:45** 4. **3:30**

► What time is it now?

5. **?**

FIND OUT HOURS

7 ► Listen to the telephone conversation.
► Act out the conversation. Call one of the places in the guidebook below.

A (*Dials number*) Rrring, rrring
B Belle Monde Restaurant, may I help you?
A Yes. What time do you open?
B We're open from 6 p.m. to midnight.
A So you open at six o'clock?
B Yes.
A O.K. Thank you.

on Mondays = every Monday

a.m. = in the morning
p.m. = in the afternoon
       in the evening
       at night

NEW ORLEANS

MUSEUMS

The Voodoo Museum
724 Dumaine Street
10:00 a.m. – 5:00 p.m.
Closed Mondays

The Art Museum
110 Rampart Street
10:00 – 5:30 every day

The Louisiana State Museum
701 Chartres Street
9:00 – 4:00, Tuesday
              to Saturday
11:00 – 3:00, Sunday
9:00 – 12:00, Monday

NEW ORLEANS

MUSIC CLUBS

The Savoy
122 Bourbon Street
Toots Bixler and his
jazz band.
9:00 p.m. to 2:00 a.m.
Closed Sunday

The Music Hall
Good old Rock and Roll
7:30 to Midnight
every night
344 Royal Street

RESTAURANTS

The Belle Monde
400 Esplanade Avenue
6:00 p.m. to Midnight
Closed Mondays
Great French food
Expensive

Italian Villa
560 Bourbon Street
Noon – Midnight every day
Good and inexpensive

12. Do you want to go to a movie?

TALK ABOUT MOVIES • SUBJECT QUESTIONS

1 ▶ **Answer the questions using the information in the movie ads.**

1. What's playing this week?
2. Who's in *The Doctor's Office*?
3. Who's in *Love on a Rainy Afternoon*?
4. Who's David Contreras?
5. What's playing at the Baker Street Theater?
6. What's playing at midnight?
7. Who's in *Rock and Roll Cowboy*?
8. What's "the best science fiction movie in years"?

> **Subject questions with who and what**
>
> **What**'s playing? ***The Lost Galaxy*** (is playing).
> **Who**'s in *Rock and Roll Cowboy*? **Charlie Mills and Donna Sue Parker.**

 2 ▶ **Listen and say *true* or *false*.**

1. *The Doctor's Office* is playing at the Baker Street Theater. *False.*
2. *The Lost Galaxy* is a great adventure movie.
3. *Casablanca* starts at midnight.
4. Tessa Lake is in *Texas Charlie and the Last Frontier*.
5. The State Theater is on Monument Avenue.
6. The Circle Cinema is downtown.
7. *Rock and Roll Cowboy* is a comedy.

3 ▶ **Talk with your classmates.**

Name a film for each category. Use the movie ads above or talk about movies you know.

Some kinds of movies	
classic movies	comedies
horror movies	dramas
adventure movies	westerns
love stories	science fiction movies
documentaries	

TALK ABOUT LIKES AND DISLIKES

4 ▶ Complete the conversation with the objections in the box. Use the information in the ads.
▶ Listen to check your answers.

A Let's go to a movie. *Casablanca* starts at midnight.
B _I don't really like old movies_ . Besides, that's too late.
A O.K. *Claws II* is at the Circle Cinema.
B The Circle is too far away and _____ .
A How about *The Story of Civilization*?
B That's too long and _____ .
A Oh, look! *Love on a Rainy Afternoon* is at the Baker Street Theater.
B _____ .
A Well, what kind of movies *do* you like?
B _____ .

> **Some polite objections**
>
> I don't really like documentaries.
> I don't really like love stories.
> I don't really like movies.
> I don't really like horror movies.
> I don't really like old movies.

5 ▶ Listen to the conversation.
▶ Have a similar conversation with a partner.

A What kind of movies do you like?
B I like horror movies. How about you?
A I like love stories.

TALK ABOUT FEELINGS • PLACEMENT OF ADJECTIVES

6 ▶ Imagine you are at a movie theater with a friend. Listen to the possible conversations.

A Are you having a good time?

B Yeah, I'm having a wonderful time.
A *I'm* not. This movie is horrible.

B No, I'm having a terrible time.
A I am too. This is an awful movie.

> **Placement of adjectives**
>
> This movie is **fantastic**.
> This is a **fantastic** movie.

> **Some adjectives**
>
> | | |
> |---|---|
> | fantastic | horrible |
> | wonderful | awful |
> | excellent | terrible |
> | good | lousy |

7 ▶ Listen to this conversation. Then act it out with a partner.

A (*Dials number*) Rrring, rrring
B Hello.
A Hi, Jeff. It's Nabila. Do you want to go to a movie?
B O.K., but I don't have a newspaper. What's playing?
A Let's see. . . . *Rock and Roll Cowboy* is playing at the Palace.
B Oh, I don't really like westerns.
A How about *The Doctor's Office*?
B Who's in it?
A Drew Young and Julia Williams.
B What time does it start?
A There are shows at 7:15 and 9:30.
B Hmm. The 9:30 show is too late. Let's go to the 7:15 show.
A O.K.

8 ▶ Play these roles.

Student A Telephone Student B and suggest going to a movie. Use the information in the movie ads or your own newspaper to answer his or her questions.

Student B Student A calls to invite you to a movie. You don't have a newspaper. Ask for more information about the movies. Agree with or object to Student A's suggestions.

13. Two tickets, please.

The Arnos go to a movie to get out of their cold apartment.

1

George It's freezing in here! What's wrong with the heat anyway?

Loretta I've got an idea. Why don't we go out?

George Out? In this weather? It's snowing!

Loretta I mean let's go somewhere warm . . . a movie, for instance. I think *Casablanca* is playing at the theater down the street.

George *Casablanca*! You know I don't like old movies!

Loretta Oh, George!

George Really, Loretta, I . . .

Loretta Come on, George. It'll be nice and warm in the theater . . . Let's see . . . It's a quarter after seven now. I'll call the theater and find out.

2. Listen in

It's a quarter after seven when Loretta calls the theater. Listen to the telephone recording. What time does the next show start?

3

Two, please. Are we late?

ADULTS $7.00
CHILDREN $4.00
SENIOR CIT.

The movie's just starting now, ma'am.

4. How to say it

Practice these conversations.

1. **A** I like old movies.

   B I do too.

2. **A** I like old movies.

   B Well, I don't.

3. **A** I don't like old movies.

   B Well, I do.

5

Loretta	Uh-oh . . .
George	What's wrong?
Loretta	I can't see! (*Turning to man*) Excuse me, sir—is this seat taken?
Man	Uh . . . no, it's not.
Loretta	Let's move down a seat, George.
Woman	Shh!

6. Your turn

A man and a woman are planning their evening. Act out the conversation. Refer to the movie section of a newspaper if possible.

Woman	What do you want to do tonight?
Man	_____ .
Woman	O.K. What do you want to see? Any suggestions?
Man	_____ .
Woman	No, I don't like that kind of movie.
Man	_____ .
Woman	That's fine. Do you know what time it starts?
Man	_____ .
Woman	Let's go to the last show.
Man	_____ .

7

Loretta	Oh, I just love Humphrey Bogart!
George	Yeah. Well, at least it was warm in there . . . What's that?
Loretta	Oh, I almost forgot. Remember that contest you entered last month?
George	Oh, yeah. For the free trip to Miami Beach.
Loretta	Well, this letter came today.

YAHOO! Pack your bikini, Loretta! We're going to Florida!

8. Figure it out

True or *false*?

1. It's very cold in the Arnos' apartment. *True.*
2. George wants to see *Casablanca*.
3. *Casablanca* is an old movie.
4. George likes the movie.
5. George and Loretta win a trip to Florida.

14. New Orleans: A tradition of good living

New Orleans with its famous French Quarter (Vieux Carré) is a never-ending delight for visitors as well as natives. For shopping, dining, entertainment or just the pleasures of walking and watching, there's no place like it in the world.
— The Greater New Orleans Tourist and Convention Commission

New Orleans, at the mouth of the Mississippi River, is a city over 270 years old. The French built the first town in 1718 and named it in honor of the French Duc d'Orleans. Today, New Orleans has over 600,000 people and it is an important U.S. port and center for tourism.

New Orleans is a city with a European flavor and an interesting history. In 1762, France gave New Orleans and part of its Louisiana colony to Spain. It belonged to Spain for over 30 years. Then in 1800 Napoleon Bonaparte asked Spain to return the territory to France again. In 1803 President Thomas Jefferson bought the Louisiana Territory, including New Orleans, from France. The cost: $15 million.

The city of New Orleans has a tradition of good living. Perhaps that's why many American writers, such as Tennessee Williams and William Faulkner, lived there at some time during their lives. Its restaurants are famous for French and Creole food. It has many old houses and government buildings. Jazz, a famous musical tradition in New Orleans, dates from the African–American community of the late nineteenth century. And every spring New Orleans celebrates its legendary holiday, Mardi Gras. From colorful celebrations in the streets to formal masquerade balls, it is a magical time of costumes, parades, and parties.

For more information see your travel agent or call or write:
The Greater New Orleans Tourist and Convention Commission
1520 Sugar Bowl Drive
New Orleans, LA 70112
504-566-5011

1. Read the article. Then circle the things you can find in New Orleans.

a. good shopping
b. interesting old buildings
c. good weather
d. great beaches
e. excellent restaurants
f. jazz

2. Answer these questions.

1. What two European countries were important in the history of New Orleans?
2. What famous holiday does New Orleans celebrate?

PREVIEW

FUNCTIONS/THEMES	LANGUAGE	FORMS
Talk about favorite foods Shop for food	Steak is my favorite food. I'll take these bananas.	Foods Demonstrative adjectives: *this*, *that*, *these*, *those*
Ask about prices Ask for something you want	How much are oranges? I'd like some pears, please. Do you need any onions?	*How much* *Some* and *any*
Make a shopping list	We need two pounds of chicken.	

Preview the conversations.

In the United States, fruits and vegetables are weighed in pounds. How are they weighed in your country?

Do you think these prices are expensive? How do they compare to prices in your country?

1 pound (lb.) = 453.5 grams (g)
2.2 pounds (lbs.) = 1 kilogram (kg)

15. Anything else?

 Before they leave for work, Russ and Jill Perkins talk about what they want for dinner.

A

Jill What do you want for dinner tonight?

Russ How about chicken?

Jill Anything but chicken. We always have chicken.

Russ Then let's go to a restaurant. There's a new Japanese restaurant on the corner.

Jill You know, I'd really like to stay home tonight.

Russ Well . . . how about steak?

Jill Mmm . . . that's my favorite food. And let's have a salad and some potatoes too. . . . And then some melon for dessert.

Russ Great. You buy the fruit and vegetables and I'll get the meat.

Jill O.K. I'll see you at six.

B

Jill I'd like this head of lettuce and a pound of those potatoes, please.

Clerk Anything else?

Jill Oh, let me think. . . . Do you have any melons?

Clerk What kind? I have these nice, fresh cantaloupes and those watermelons over there.

Jill The cantaloupes look good. How much are they?

Clerk They're $1.99 each.

Jill I'll take two, please.

Clerk All right. Would you like anything else?

Jill No, that's all. How much is it?

Clerk Let's see. . . . That'll be $5.47.

C

Clerk May I help you?
Russ Yes. I'd like some steak, please.
Clerk I'm sorry. I'm all out of steak.
Russ Well . . . do you have any chicken?
Clerk Sure. I always have chicken.

D

Jill I'm really hungry. Where's the steak?
Russ Well . . . they were all out of steak.
 So here's some chicken instead.
Jill Chicken?
Russ Yeah. Chicken.
Jill Russ, let's go to a restaurant.
Russ Well, how about Japanese food?
 There's a new Japanese restaurant on
 the corner, you know. . . .

Figure it out

1. Listen to the conversation and answer the questions.

1. Does Russ want to eat dinner at home?
3. Does Jill really want to eat in a restaurant?

2. Listen again. Say *true, false,* or *it doesn't say.*

1. Russ wants to eat in a restaurant. *True.*
2. The watermelons look bad.
3. Jill's favorite food is salad.
4. The store is out of chicken.
5. Russ and Jill are going to eat in a restaurant.

3. Match.

1. How about potatoes?
2. Anything else?
3. Where are the potatoes?
4. How much is it?

a. They were out of potatoes.
b. Anything but potatoes.
c. No, that's all.
d. $5.47.

16. Steak is my favorite food.

FOODS

🔊 **1** ▶ **Listen to this magazine article and find each item in the picture.**

The four basic food groups are the *Fruit and Vegetable Group*; the *Meat, Fish, and Egg Group*; the *Milk Group*; and the *Grain Group*.

The Fruit and Vegetable Group includes bananas, grapes, apples, oranges, melons, spinach, potatoes, tomatoes, carrots, lettuce, and many more. The Meat, Fish, and Egg Group contains fish, eggs, and meats such as beef, pork, lamb, chicken, and turkey. The Milk Group includes foods like milk, cheese, and yogurt. Finally, the foods in the Grain Group are breads, pastas (like spaghetti), and cereals.

2 ▶ **Answer these questions.**

1. Name three kinds of fruit.
2. Name three vegetables.
3. Which of the foods in the article do you eat? Which of these foods don't you eat?
4. Which foods do you think are good for you and which ones do you think are bad for you?

3 ▶ **Interview your classmates. Ask about each student's favorite foods.**

A What's your favorite fruit?
B Apples.

A What's your favorite vegetable?
B Carrots.

4 ▶ **Study the frame.**

Demonstrative adjectives	
I'll take	**this** banana.
	these bananas.
I don't want	**that** banana.
	those bananas.

5 ▶ **Fill in the blanks with *this, that, these,* or *those*.**
▶ **Listen to check your answers.**

A O.K. What do we need?
B Bananas, apples, and watermelon.
A Well, _____ bananas look terrible.
B Yeah, but _____ bananas are ripe. And _____ watermelon is fresh, too.
A What about the apples?
B Ugh . . . look! _____ apples are rotten!
A Yuk! Let's take _____ apples instead.

6 ▶ **Compare the fruit at the two stands.**

This watermelon is 49¢ a pound. That watermelon is 45¢ a pound.
These apples are rotten. Those apples are fresh.
These bananas are ripe. Those bananas are too ripe.

49¢ lb. = forty-nine cents a pound.

Some adjectives	
fresh	old
rotten	ripe

17. How much are oranges?

1 ▶ Listen to the radio ad. Find the items in the picture.

▶ Listen again. There are two mistakes in the radio ad. What are they?

▶ Ask and answer questions like the ones below.

1. How much is a bag of potatoes?
2. How much are tomatoes?
3. How much are oranges?
4. How much are bananas?
5. How much is salmon?
6. How much is chicken?
7. How much are these things at your local market?

55¢ ea. = fifty-five cents each
3/$1 = three for a dollar

potato + es ➔ potatoes
tomato + es ➔ tomatoes

Nick's Grocery
S P E C I A L   S A L E

VEGETABLES
Potatoes $2.49 *5 lb. bag*
Tomatoes 89¢ lb.
Head of Lettuce 99¢
Head of Garlic $1.29 lb.
Onions 59¢ lb.

F R U I T S
Oranges 3/$1
Bananas 89¢ lb.
Pears 79¢ lb.
Watermelon 49¢ lb.
Grapes 99¢ lb.
Apples 55¢ lb.

M E A T S
Pork Chops $2.29 lb.
Lamb Chops $3.19 lb.
Chicken $2.49 lb.
Ground Beef $2.29 lb.

F I S H
Salmon $7.99 lb.
Flounder $5.99 lb.

chicken   pork   beef   lamb   turkey   fish

Sale Starts March 3 and Ends March 8

2 ▶ Study the frame.

Some and any

I have	**some**	onions.
I don't have	**any**	
Do you have	**any**	onions?

Some is used in polite requests:

*Would you like **some** onions?*

3 ▶ Complete the conversation with *some* or *any*.

▶ Listen to check your work.

A I'd like ___*some*___ pears, please.
B I'm sorry. I don't have _____ pears.
A Do you have _____ apples?
B Yes. I have _____ nice apples.
A Great. I'll take three, please.
B O.K. Anything else?
A Yes. I'd like _____ bananas too.
B Sure. They're 89¢ a pound.
A O.K. Give me six, please.

ASK FOR SOMETHING YOU WANT

4 ▶ **Listen to the possible conversations.**
▶ **Imagine you are at Nick's Grocery. Act out the conversation with a partner.**

A May I help you?

B Yes. I'd like two pounds of tomatoes, please.

A Anything else?

B Yes, do you have any onions?

A No. I'm all out of onions.

B O.K. That's all then.

A Let's see. . . . That'll be $1.78.

A Yes, they're right over here.

B Great. Give me a pound, please.

A Let's see. . . . That'll be $2.37.

You can say:

I'll take	
I'd like	two pounds, please.
Give me	

I'd like . . . is more polite than *I want . . .*

MAKE A SHOPPING LIST

5 ▶ **Listen to the conversation.**

A May I help you?
B Yes. I'd like two pounds of tomatoes, please.
A Anything else?
B Yes. I'd also like a pound of onions.
A I'm sorry. I'm all out of onions.
B Oh . . . do you have any garlic?
A Yes, it's right over here.
B O.K. I'll take a head of garlic.
A Would you like anything else?
B Yes. I'd like a watermelon, please.
A Sure. That'll be $6.20.

▶ **Have similar conversations using the shopping lists.**

1.
Shopping List
2 lbs. tomatoes
1 lb. onions
1 head garlic
1 watermelon

Sorry — We're out of:
onions   potatoes
grapes   pork chops

3.
Shopping List
3 lbs. ground beef
1 lb. chicken
1 lb. bananas
2 lbs. pork chops

2.
Shopping List
4 bananas
1 lb. grapes
2 cantaloupes
2 lbs. apples

---

6 ▶ **A woman is shopping at Nick's Grocery. Listen to the conversation and check the items she buys.**

Shopping List

____ 1 lb. tomatoes
____ 1 bag of potatoes
____ 1 head of lettuce
____ 1 lb. onions
____ 8 apples
____ 2 lbs. pears
____ 6 oranges

7 ▶ **Listen to the conversation.**

A What do you want for dinner?
B Let's have chicken.
C How much is it?
D It's $2.49 a pound at Nick's Grocery.
B O.K. We need two pounds. That'll be about $5.00.
A What kind of vegetable do you want? . . .

▶ **Solve this problem.**

Work in groups of four. Imagine you are preparing dinner tonight and you have only $10.00 for food. Agree on what food to buy from Nick's Grocery and make a shopping list.

18. Department store

Loretta is shopping for a bathing suit with Stella.

1

Clerk May I help you?

Loretta Yes. I'm going to Florida and I need a new bathing suit.

Clerk Well, we have some very nice bathing suits right over here. I'm sure we have one just for you. What size do you wear — a twelve?

Loretta *(Laughs)* No. I need a fourteen.

Clerk The fourteens are over here. . . . This is beautiful, don't you think?

Stella Oh, that *is* pretty, Loretta.

Loretta No. I don't like all those flowers.

Clerk But that's the style this year. Everyone's wearing flowers.

Loretta Well, not me!

2

Stella How about those over there?

Clerk Those are bikinis.

Loretta *(Laughing)* Me in a bikini? I don't think so.

Clerk Well, do you like this?

Loretta Hmm . . . that's not bad. What do you think, Stella?

Stella Oh, it's very nice. I like it.

Loretta How much is it?

Clerk $59.98.

Loretta Oh, no. That's too expensive for . . .

Stella Oh, come on, Loretta. Try it on!

3

Loretta Well? What do you think?

Stella You look terrific! George is going to love it!

Loretta O.K. I'll take it.

How is it?

Just a minute.

4. Figure it out

True, false, or *it doesn't say*?

1. Loretta wants a new bathing suit for Florida.
2. Loretta wants a bikini.
3. George likes bathing suits with lots of flowers.
4. Loretta tries on a bathing suit with flowers.
5. Loretta buys a bathing suit for $59.98.

5. Listen in

Some people are shopping for different things in a big department store. Look at the pictures. Then match the appropriate picture (*a*, *b*, *c*, or *d*) with each conversation you hear.

1. First conversation _____
2. Second conversation _____
3. Third conversation _____
4. Fourth conversation _____

Notebooks
6 for $5.00

a.

NEW RELEASES

VIDEO CENTER

b.

c.

d.

6. How to say it

Practice this conversation.

A I like the red sunglasses. How much are they?

B $14.95. (fourteen ninety-five)

A And those?

B $12.95. (twelve ninety-five)

7. Your turn

A customer in the department store wants to buy some brown sunglasses. Act out a possible conversation between the customer and the clerk.

Clerk	May I help you?
Customer	_____
Clerk	These?
Customer	_____
Clerk	Oh, those . . . Here you are.
Customer	_____
Clerk	They're $15.50.
Customer	_____
Clerk	Anything else?
Customer	_____
Clerk	O.K. That'll be $15.50.

19. World Travelers

1 It grows best in hot, wet weather and young plants usually grow in fields under water. It originally comes from India and China where it grew 3,000 to 5,000 years ago. Today it also grows in North and South America, but more than 95% of the world's supply comes from Southeast Asia. We only eat the seeds of this plant, but you have to cook them.

peanut

2 In the sixteenth century, Spanish explorers found them in Peru and took them back to Spain. At about the same time, Sir Walter Raleigh introduced them to England and Ireland. People have to wash them very well because they grow under the ground. Today, the French style of cooking them is very popular and North America, Northern Europe, and the former Soviet Union are the biggest producers.

rice

3 Peru was their native home, but they first became an important food in Mexico. Spanish explorers took them from South America to Europe, but most Europeans would not eat them. They thought they were poisonous. Today people eat them raw or cooked, and they are very popular in Italian cooking. The United States, Italy, Spain, Brazil, and Japan are the major producers of this food.

banana

4 Originally, they grew wild in the tropical jungles of Asia. They traveled across the islands of the Pacific and also across the Indian Ocean to Africa. Later they traveled across the Atlantic to the West Indies and America. You cut them when they are green, then they ripen and turn yellow and sweet. They are delicious raw, but you can also cook them. Central and South America and the West Indies grow them for export.

potato

5 One interesting story is that Spanish explorers found them in South America in the sixteenth century and took them back to Spain. At about the same time, explorers probably carried them from South America across the Pacific to China. The Spanish and Portuguese traded them in Africa for spices and elephant tusks. When slave ships went from Africa to North America, this food went back to America. Today, China, parts of Africa, and the United States grow most of them.

tomato

1. Read the article and match the descriptions with the names under the pictures.

2. Answer the questions.

1. Which three foods are originally from South America?
2. Which two are from Asia?

PREVIEW

FUNCTIONS/THEMES	LANGUAGE	FORMS
Talk about past activities	They visited their friends. They went to the ballet	The past tense
Ask about the weekend	How was your weekend?	
Ask about the past	What did you do?	Information questions in the past tense
Talk about the past	She went to the office. She was at the office. She was in the office.	*To, at, in* with the definite article

Preview the conversations.

On Saturday night, Jenny and Sherry went to a movie. What movie did they see? What did they do after the movie?

20. Saturday night . . .

Jenny and her friend Sherry see *Gone with the Wind* for the third time.

A

Jenny Well, what did you think of the movie?

Sherry Oh, it was wonderful! I loved it!

Jenny Me too. I'd like to see it again.

Sherry Yeah, it's a classic. So, do you want to get some ice cream?

Jenny Sure.

B

Sherry So, are you still working at the Stop and Shop?

Jenny Just on Mondays and Wednesdays. Do you know who works there now? Gary Selby.

Sherry No kidding! I saw him last week at a party. He's a pretty nice guy.

Jenny Yeah, he is.

C

Jenny How was your weekend?

Gary It was pretty boring, actually. I visited my parents on Saturday and I studied all day yesterday. Last night I was tired so I went to bed early. How about you? What did you do?

Jenny Sherry and I went out Saturday night.

Gary So, what did you do?

Jenny Oh, we went to the movies.

Gary What did you see?

Jenny We saw *Gone with the Wind*.

Gary Oh, I saw that last year. I didn't like it much, though.

Jenny Really? Why not?

Gary I guess I just don't like romantic movies.

Figure it out

1. Listen to the conversation. Then complete the sentences with *good* or *boring*.

Jenny's weekend was pretty _____ .
Gary's weekend was pretty _____ .

2. Listen again and answer *true, false,* or *it doesn't say*.

1. Jenny and Sherry went out Saturday night.
2. They had a pizza before the movie.
3. They thought the movie was great.
4. They got ice cream after the movie.
5. Jenny worked on Sunday.
6. Sherry knows Gary.
7. Gary studied on Sunday.
8. Both Jenny and Gary liked *Gone with the Wind*.

3. Match each verb with its past form.

1. ask   a. got
2. have   b. asked
3. study   c. did
4. go   d. studied
5. do   e. saw
6. see   f. had
7. love   g. went
8. get   h. loved

21. How was your weekend?

1 ► **Listen to what the people in the pictures did yesterday.**
► **Match the descriptions with the pictures.**

1. He had dinner with a friend.
2. She got ice cream.
3. They went to the ballet.
4. She did her homework.
5. He lost his wallet.

6. She visited her parents.
7. They studied at the library.
8. She worked all day.
9. He relaxed at home.
10. They watched TV.

2 ▶ **Study the frames: Past Tense**

Affirmative statements			
I	**liked**	[t]	the movie a lot.
We			
She	**studied**	[d]	French last night.
He			
They	**visited**	[əd]	their friends yesterday.

Past tense of regular verbs		
like + **ed**	➡	**liked**
visit + **ed**	➡	**visited**
study + **ed**	➡	**studied**

Some irregular verbs			
do	**did**	have	**had**
get	**got**	lose	**lost**
go	**went**		

They **went** to the beach.

3 ▶ **Gary's weekend was boring, but the weekend before last, he had more fun. Complete the conversation using the information in the pictures.**
▶ **Listen to check your answers.**

Jim How was your weekend, Gary?
Gary Oh, it was pretty good. On Friday night _____ .
Jim How about Saturday?
Gary Well, in the morning _____ . On Saturday night _____ .
Jim Sunday night too?
Gary No, _____ .

Friday 11:30 PM

Saturday 11:00 AM

Saturday 10:00 PM

Sunday 8:00 PM

4 ▶ **Talk with your classmates. Ask about their weekend.**

22. What did you do?

1 ► Complete the paragraphs about Jenny's mother, Mrs. Wilcox. Use the
past tense of the verbs in parentheses.
► Listen to check your work.

Mrs. Wilcox _____ (have) a terrible day on Monday. You see, her
entire life is in her appointment book and she _____ (lose) it.

She _____ (go) to Chicago for a business meeting. At the meeting, she
looked in her briefcase for her appointment book, but it wasn't there.
She _____ (think) maybe she _____ (put) it in her handbag, but it
wasn't there either.

After her meeting she _____ (have) dinner and _____ (see) a movie.
Then she returned to the hotel. At the hotel she _____ (get) a surprise. There was a message from the
airline. They _____ (say) they _____ (find) her appointment book. She _____ (leave) it on the plane.

Some more irregular verbs			
find	**found**	see	**saw**
leave	**left**	take	**took**
put	**put**	think	**thought**
say	**said**		

2 ► Look at Mrs. Wilcox's appointment book. Answer the questions.

1. Where did she go on Sunday afternoon?
2. What time did she have a meeting at City Bank?
3. What did she do Monday evening?

4. Where did she go on Tuesday?
5. Who did she see?
6. What did she do on Friday?

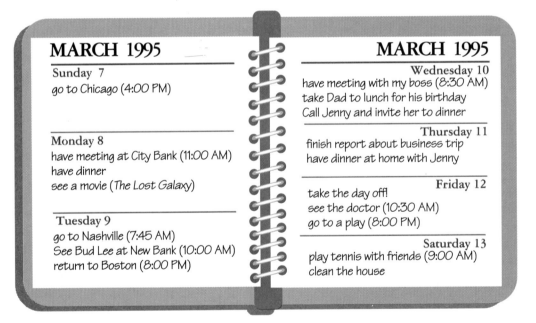

MARCH 1995
Sunday 7
go to Chicago (4:00 PM)

Monday 8
have meeting at City Bank (11:00 AM)
have dinner
see a movie (The Lost Galaxy)

Tuesday 9
go to Nashville (7:45 AM)
See Bud Lee at New Bank (10:00 AM)
return to Boston (8:00 PM)

MARCH 1995
Wednesday 10
have meeting with my boss (8:30 AM)
take Dad to lunch for his birthday
Call Jenny and invite her to dinner

Thursday 11
finish report about business trip
have dinner at home with Jenny

Friday 12
take the day off!
see the doctor (10:30 AM)
go to a play (8:00 PM)

Saturday 13
play tennis with friends (9:00 AM)
clean the house

3 ► Study the frame: Information Questions
in the Past Tense

4 ► Imagine it's Saturday. Ask and answer
questions about Mrs. Wilcox's week.

Information questions						
Where			**go?**		**went** to Nashville.	
What	**did**	you	**do?**	I	**had** a meeting.	
Who			**see?**		**saw** Bud Lee.	

Expressions in the past	
Monday morning	last Monday
yesterday afternoon	yesterday evening
last night	last weekend

23. Yesterday

 1 ▶ **Jenny is talking to her friend Sherry. Listen and check the things she did yesterday.**

1. _____ She went to the hospital.
2. _____ She took some books to a friend.
3. _____ She did her homework in the hospital.
4. _____ She had lunch with her mother at home.
5. _____ She went shopping.
6. _____ She looked for a new wallet.
7. _____ She got a new watch.
8. _____ She went to class.

2 ▶ **Study the frame and look at the pictures.**

To, at, and *in* with the definite article

| She went | to | **the** office.
the hospital.
work.
school.
class. | She was | at | **the** office.
the hospital.
work.
school.
home. |
| | | home. | | in | **the** office.
the hospital.
class. |

She went to the hospital.

She was at the hospital.

She was in the hospital.

3 ▶ **Complete the paragraph with *to (the)*, *at (the)*, or *in (the)* if necessary.**

Jenny's friend Mark was _____ hospital. On Tuesday Jenny went _____ hospital to visit him. She was _____ hospital for an hour. Then she went _____ work. She was _____ work all day. After work she went shopping and then at six o'clock she went _____ class. Finally, at eight thirty she went _____ home.

4 ▶ **Interview a classmate.**

Find out what a classmate did yesterday. Use the questions in the box or your own questions. Tell another classmate about your partner.

Where were you yesterday?
What did you do there?
Where were you last night?
What did you do/see/have? Anything exciting?

24. Now think back . . .

George and Loretta arrive at the airport.

1

George	What did you put in these suitcases, lead?
Loretta	I'm sorry, George. We had a lot of things.
Employee	May I help you?
Loretta	Yes. We're going to Miami.
Employee	May I see your tickets, please?
Loretta	George . . .
George	Huh?
Loretta	Give her the tickets.
George	Oh, the tickets . . . uh–oh . . .
Loretta	What's the matter?
George	I don't have the tickets.

2

Loretta	You don't have the tickets! George, it's two thirty. The flight leaves in half an hour!
George	Now calm down, Loretta.
Loretta	O.K. . . . I gave them to you this morning, remember?
George	Right.
Loretta	At breakfast.
George	Right.
Loretta	Now think back. What did you do after that?
George	Let's see . . . I got up from the table . . .
Loretta	Yes . . .
George	. . . and I went into the bedroom . . .
Loretta	Yes . . .
George	. . . and I put them in the pocket of my jacket . . . and now they're not there. (*George looks in his pocket.*)
Loretta	That's not possible, George. Look again.
George	Wait! Now I remember! I put them in the pocket of my *blue* jacket! It's in my suitcase.

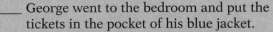

3. Figure it out

Now think back and put the events in the correct order.

_____ George went to the bedroom and put the tickets in the pocket of his blue jacket.
_____ Loretta gave George the tickets.
_____ George remembered that the tickets were in the pocket of his blue jacket.
_____ George and Loretta found the tickets.
_____ Loretta asked George for the tickets.
_____ George and Loretta went to the airport.
_____ George put his blue jacket in his suitcase.
_____ The tickets weren't in George's pocket.

🔊 4. Listen in

A man is saying good-bye to a woman at the airport. Read the questions below. Then listen to the conversation and answer the questions.

1. Where is the woman going?
2. Where did the man's sister go?

5. Your turn

George finds the tickets and shows them to Loretta. She is very relieved and happy. Act out the conversation.

🔊 6. How to say it

Listen to the conversation below. Then practice it.

A Where <u>did</u> <u>you</u> go?   [diʤuw]
B To Chicago.
A What <u>did</u> <u>you</u> do there?   [diʤuw]
B I visited some friends.
A When <u>did</u> <u>you</u> get back?   [diʤuw]
B Last night.

7. Your turn

Amy runs into her friend Lou in the airport. They were both away on trips. Act out the conversation.

Amy Lou! How are you doing?
Lou _____
Amy So, where were you this time?
Lou _____
Amy London.
Lou _____
Amy Oh, my trip was O.K. By the way, Ellen Mason was on the flight.
Lou _____
Amy She's fine. She says hello.

Tomorrow Is Another Day

On December 15, 1939, Rhett Butler and Scarlett O'Hara came alive on the movie screen. From the very first moment, people fell in love with a movie about life in the Old South. Based on Margaret Mitchell's 1936 novel, it is the story of a self-centered young woman who struggles to live through the American Civil War, but then loses the only man she loves.

Clark Gable was everyone's choice to play Rhett Butler. Thousands of people sent letters to the movie studio saying that Clark Gable was perfect for the part. Gable was not interested, but he had to take the part because he had a contract at the studio.

It was more difficult for Selznick to find a

When Margaret Mitchell was 35, she found herself at home in Atlanta with a broken ankle and nothing to do. She had read all of the books in the local library so her husband suggested that she write her own book. Its original title was Tomorrow Is Another Day. *When it was published, more than 100,000 copies sold immediately. It became a best-seller and David O. Selznick at the MGM movie studio bought the movie rights. Mitchell never wanted to write a sequel to her novel. For her, she said, the story had ended. She died in 1949 before anyone could change her mind. In 1991,* Scarlett, *a novel by Alexandra Ripley, was published with the approval of Margaret Mitchell's estate.*

female lead. Everyone tested for the part, from Lucille Ball to Joan Crawford. A young British actress named Vivien Leigh was in Hollywood visiting her boyfriend, the famous actor Lawrence Olivier. Selznick's brother Myron was Olivier's agent. When Myron Selznick met Vivien Leigh, he knew immediately that she would be the ideal Scarlett O'Hara. So he developed a plan. He arranged for her to meet David O. Selznick. For the meeting she wore a large hat and green eye shadow. Myron introduced her to David as Scarlett O'Hara. She got the part.

The movie won eight Academy Awards, including best picture, best performance by an actress (Vivien Leigh), and best performance by a supporting actress (Hattie McDaniel, the first African-American actor to receive an Oscar). The movie's spectacular sets, romantic costumes, and dramatic music make it as popular today as it was more than fifty years ago.

1. **What is the real name of this famous novel and movie?**

2. **Answer these questions.**

1. Who wrote the original novel?
2. Why did Clark Gable take the part?
3. Who played Scarlett O'Hara? Where was the actress from?
4. Is there a sequel to the novel? Who wrote it?

Review of Units 1-4

1 ▸ You are calling a friend who has moved to Los Angeles. Complete the phone conversation.
▸ Imagine your partner moved to one of the cities in the weather report. Act out a similar conversation.

A _____
B Oh, pretty good. How are you?
A _____
B Nothing much. I'm just sitting here and reading a book, and I decided to call you.
A _____
B Yes. I like Los Angeles a lot.
A _____
B It's very hot today. So, what are you doing now?
A _____

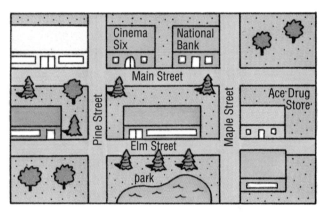

WEATHER REPORT			
Athens	65°		cloudy
Cairo	95°		sunny
Helsinki	20°		snowing
London	72°		raining
Los Angeles	86°		sunny
Madrid	50°		windy
Moscow	40°		cloudy
Seoul	55°		raining

2A ▸ Student A follows the instructions below. Student B follows the instructions on page B44.

Student A Ask your partner if there's a *department store*, a *bookstore*, a *shoe store*, and a *grocery store* in the neighborhood shown on the map. Locate the places if they exist. Then answer your partner's questions.

3A ▸ Student A follows the instructions below. Student B follows the instructions on page B44.

Student A You and your partner are coming out of the elevators in Brennan's Department Store. Ask your partner for directions to the *cafeteria*, the *restrooms*, the *drinking fountain*, and the *stairs*. Locate each place on the floor plan. Then answer your partner's questions.

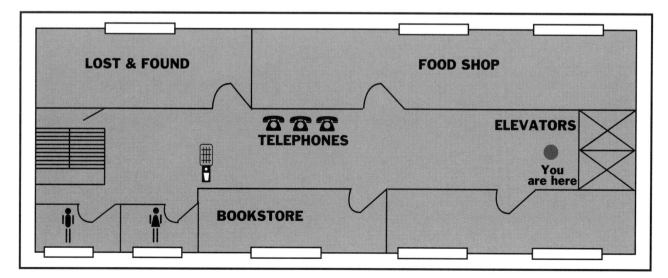

2B ▶ **Student B follows the instructions below. Student A follows the instructions on page B43.**

Student B Use the map to answer your partner's questions. Then ask your partner if there's a *video store*, a *drugstore*, a *bank*, and a *movie theater* in the neighborhood. Locate the places on the map.

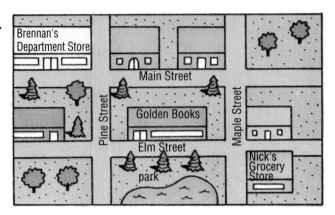

3B ▶ **Student B follows the instructions below. Student A follows the instructions on page B43.**

Student B You and your partner are coming out of the elevators in Brennan's Department Store. Answer your partner's questions. Then ask your partner for directions to the *food shop*, the *telephones*, the *bookstore*, and the *Lost and Found*. Locate each place on the floor plan.

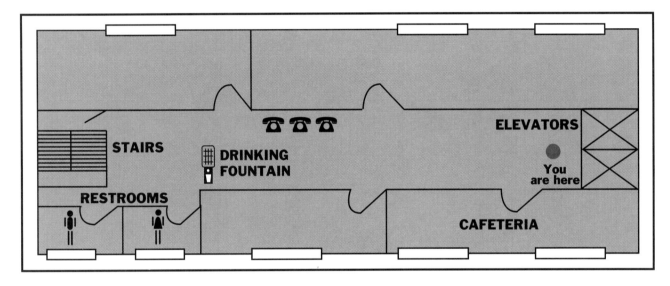

4 ▶ Listen to the radio commercial for Brennan's Department Store. Then complete the newspaper ad with the correct address and store hours.

5 ► **You are in the men's department of Brennan's. Look at the picture and complete the conversation.**

  ► **Act out a similar conversation with a partner, talking about other items in the picture.**

Customer Excuse me, how much are these silk ties?
Salesperson _____
Customer Oh, they're too expensive.
Salesperson _____
Customer Yes. They are pretty nice. How much are they?
Salesperson _____
Customer Good. I'll take a blue tie and a green tie.
Salesperson _____
Customer No. That's all. How much is it?
Salesperson _____

6 ► **You are standing at the sale table in the men's department. Compare the items on the table with those on the counter.**

These ties are cotton.
Those ties are silk.

These wallets are $3.50.
Those wallets are $10.00.

7 ► **Complete the conversation.**

A _____
B What's wrong?
A _____
B Your sweater? It's over there on the teacher's desk.
A _____

8 ► **Play a game.**

Your partner will hide one of your personal belongings. Act out a conversation like the one on the left.

9 ▶ You are in the food shop at Brennan's. Complete the conversation.
  ▶ Look at the picture and act out a similar conversation with a partner.

You Excuse me. Do you have any pears?
Clerk _____
You Oh, no! Well, give me six oranges instead.
Clerk _____
You No. That's all.
Clerk _____

10 ▶ Imagine you are having coffee at Brennan's cafeteria and you see a friend. Greet your friend and ask about his or her weekend. Tell about your weekend. Use the sentences in the box.

How was your weekend?
What did you do?

11 ▶ Complete the conversation.

A Let's go to a movie.
B _____
A *Gone with the Wind* is playing at the Winthrop.
B _____
A How about *Sylvia's Adventures*? It's playing at the Cinema Center.
B _____
A There are shows at 8:20 and 10:30.
B _____
A O.K.

▶ Act out a similar conversation with a partner. Suggest going to see a movie shown in the ad or one advertised in your local newspaper.

GLOBAL CINEMAS

Original 3 hour classic
GONE WITH THE WIND
WINTHROP THEATER•at 7:00 and 10:00
3rd Ave & 60th St. • 555-6754

A very funny comedy – ★★★1/2
SYLVIA'S ADVENTURES
CINEMA CENTER 1 • at 8:20 and 10:30

THE LOVE STORY OF THE YEAR
Uncommon Love
CINEMA CENTER 2 • at 8:30 and 10:10
52 W. 8th St. • 555-6515

Science Fiction – Experience the Future...
Creature From Outer Space
STATE THEATER • at 7:15 and 9:45
34 St. at 3rd Ave. • 555-7316

A Classic Western – ★★★★
✳ Sunset Trails ✳
PALACE • at 10:00 and Midnight
22 Sutton Place • 555-4769

PREVIEW

FUNCTIONS/THEMES	LANGUAGE	FORMS
Make small talk	Nice day.	*There is* and *there are*
Talk about places to live Give an opinion	I live in the city. There's always something to do. In my opinion, it's the only place to live.	
Talk about favorite cities	New York is my favorite city.	
Talk about likes and dislikes	Robert likes classical music, and I do too. Robert doesn't like mystery novels, and I don't either.	Rejoinders: *too* and *either*
Talk about what you have in common	How old are you? Twenty-five. Oh, I am too! I love nightclubs. But the nightclubs here are awful.	Nouns with and without *the*

Preview the conversations.

In your country, if you don't know someone and want to start a conversation, how do you begin?

26. In my opinion . . .

Two strangers on their lunch hour are talking in the park in New York City.

A

Todd Nice day.
Kim Yeah, it is.
Todd Don't you work at the Plaza Hotel?
Kim Uh-huh.
Todd I thought so. Me too. I just started there last week.

B

Todd Do you live here in the city?
Kim No. I live in the country.
Todd Oh? Where?
Kim Cold Spring. It's a small town about an hour from here.
Todd That's pretty far.
Kim I know, but I like the country. It's very quiet — especially after a long day at work.
Todd How do you get to work?
Kim I take the train. It takes me about an hour.

C

Kim Where do *you* live?
Todd Here in the city.
Kim Do you like it?
Todd Yeah. In my opinion, it's the only place to live.
Kim Why do you say that?
Todd Because there's always something to do and it's never boring.
Kim But the country isn't boring either. You can swim, fish, hike, have a garden — all kinds of things.
Todd I guess.

D

Todd What are you reading?
Kim It's a new book by Robert Ludlum.
Todd Oh, he's great.
Kim I agree. I like most mystery writers, but Ludlum's my favorite.

E

Todd So, what kind of music do you like?
Kim Most kinds. Rock, rap, jazz…
Todd Me too, but I like classical music best.
Kim Oh, that's the only kind of music I don't like. It puts me to sleep.

Figure it out

1. Listen to the conversation and answer *true* or *false*.

1. The man and the woman both like mystery writers.
2. The man and the woman both like classical music.

2. Match.

1. Do you live here in the city?
2. Nice day.
3. Where do you live?
4. Why do you say that?
5. Oh, he's a good writer.
6. What kind of music do you like?

a. Most kinds.
b. Because it's never boring.
c. No.
d. Yes, it is.
e. Here in the city.
f. I agree.

27. Nice day

1 ▶ **Listen to the conversation.**
▶ **Start a conversation and find out about someone you don't know very well.**

A Beautiful day.
B Yes, it is.
A Do you work near here?
B Uh-huh. On Fifth Avenue.
A And do you live here in the city?
B No. I live in the country.
A How do you get to work?
B I take the train. It takes about an hour.

Beautiful day.

Awful day.

I take the train.　I take the subway.　I ride my motorcycle.

I take the bus.　I ride my bike.　I walk.　I drive.

TALK ABOUT PLACES TO LIVE • GIVE AN OPINION • *THERE IS* AND *THERE ARE*

2 ▶ **Listen to the conversation. Put an *M* in front of the things the man likes about the city.**
▶ **Listen again. Put a *W* in front of the woman's opinions about the city.**

Some Opinions

There's always something to do.	There's nothing to do.
There are a lot of great restaurants.	There aren't many good restaurants.
There are discos.	There aren't any discos.
There are excellent museums.	There aren't any museums.
There are a lot of trees and flowers.	There aren't many trees and flowers.
It's exciting.	It's boring.
It's safe.	It's dangerous.
It's too quiet.	It's too noisy.
It's clean.	It's dirty.
It's cheap.	It's expensive.

3 ▶ **Listen to these possible conversations.**
▶ **Have a similar conversation with a partner.**

A Do you live here in the city?
B Uh-huh.
A Do you like it?
B Yeah. In my opinion, it's the only place to live. There's always something to do.
A I agree. It's very exciting.

A Do you live here in the city?
B No. I live in the country about an hour from here.
A Do you like it?
B Not really. In my opinion, it's boring.
A Oh, I disagree. There are lots of things to do in the country.

the city

the suburbs

a small town

the country

4 ▶ **Study the frames.**

There is and *there are*		
There	**is**	always something to do.
	isn't	anything to do.
	are	excellent museums.
	aren't	any discos.

Is	**there**	a zoo in New York City?	Yes, **there is.** No, **there isn't.**
Are		any good restaurants?	Yes, **there are.** No, **there aren't.**

5 ▶ **Listen to the conversation.**
   ▶ **Practice the conversation with a partner.**

A New York is my favorite city.
B Why do you say that?
A Because there are great restaurants and nightclubs.
B Is there a good museum there?
A Yes, there is. There's the Museum of Modern Art.

> Why . . . ?
> Because . . .

6 ▶ **Talk to your classmates.**

Tell about your favorite city. Use the words in the box or your own information.

beautiful old houses	fantastic nightclubs
beautiful streets	great beaches
delicious food	friendly people

7 ▶ **Complete this travel ad with *there, their,* and *they're*.**

New York is Art

_____ are several very well known museums in New York City, for example, the Metropolitan Museum of Art, the Museum of Modern Art and the Guggenheim Museum. _____ all excellent and _____ exhibits change regularly. _____ open from about 10 A.M. to 5 P.M. and closed one day a week. Call first for _____ hours.

Is _____ a museum children will enjoy? Definitely. _____ is the Museum of Natural History and the Museum of the American Indian. _____ very popular with children and school groups.

28. What kind of music do you like?

TALK ABOUT LIKES AND DISLIKES • REJOINDERS *TOO* AND *EITHER*

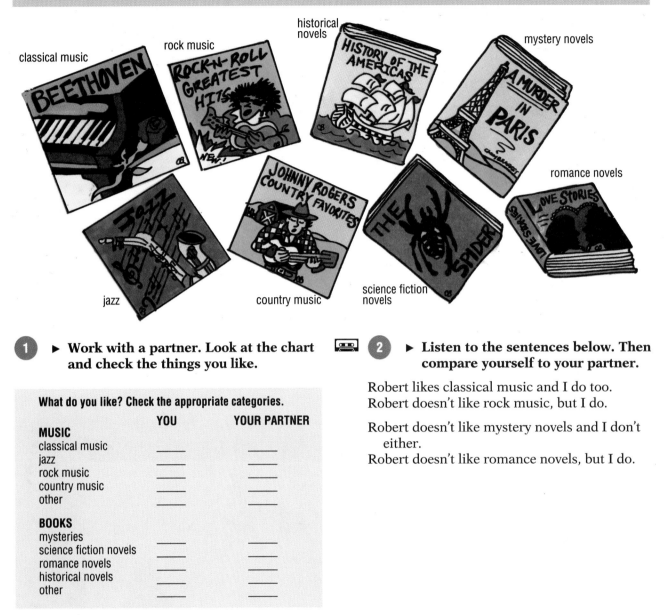

classical music
rock music
historical novels
mystery novels
romance novels
jazz
country music
science fiction novels

1 ▶ **Work with a partner. Look at the chart and check the things you like.**

What do you like? Check the appropriate categories.

	YOU	YOUR PARTNER
MUSIC		
classical music	_____	_____
jazz	_____	_____
rock music	_____	_____
country music	_____	_____
other	_____	_____
BOOKS		
mysteries	_____	_____
science fiction novels	_____	_____
romance novels	_____	_____
historical novels	_____	_____
other	_____	_____

2 ▶ **Listen to the sentences below. Then compare yourself to your partner.**

Robert likes classical music and I do too.
Robert doesn't like rock music, but I do.

Robert doesn't like mystery novels and I don't either.
Robert doesn't like romance novels, but I do.

3 ▶ **Study the frames.**

Rejoinders with *too*			
I'm single.	I He She	am is	**too.**
I'm reading a book.	We They	are	
He likes classical music.	I We They	do	**too.**
	She	does	

Rejoinders with *either*			
I'm not married.	I He She	'm not isn't	**either.**
We're not doing anything.	We They	aren't	
She doesn't like jazz.	I We They	don't	**either.**
	She	doesn't	

4 ▶ **John and Mary find out they have a lot in common. Complete the conversation.**
　　 ▶ **Listen to check your answers.**

Mary How old are you?
John Twenty-five.
Mary Oh, _____ . Are you married?
John No, I'm not.
Mary _____ . I have a roommate.
John _____ . We live in the suburbs.
Mary How do you get to work?
John I take the bus.
Mary _____ . I have a car, but I don't like to drive into the city.
John _____ .
Mary What kind of music do you like?
John Mostly rock. But I like rap too. In fact, I'm going to the Hammer concert tonight.
Mary _____ . Maybe I'll see you there.

5 ▶ **Put the lines of the conversation in order.**
　　 ▶ **Listen to check your answers.**

____ I like rap best.
____ I agree. Do you like classical music?
____ Oh, me too. Who's your favorite singer or group?
____ What kind of music do you like?
____ No, not really.
____ Me either. It puts me to sleep.
____ Hammer. He's great.

6 ▶ **Talk with your classmates.**

Find out what you have in common with your classmates. Ask what music and books they like.

> Me too. = I do too.
> Me either (Me neither). = I don't either.

7 ▶ **Study the pictures. Then complete the conversation with *the* where necessary.**

I love nightclubs.

But the nightclubs here are awful.

A I'm going to New York. How is _____ night life there?
B _____ night life in New York in wonderful. I really like _____ discos and nightclubs, and _____ nightclubs in New York are terrific. Do you like _____ music?
A Yeah, I always listen to _____ music, especially jazz.
B Well, _____ jazz in New York is great. Only New Orleans has better jazz clubs. You'll have a good time.

29. What a life!

Loretta and George are enjoying the sun in Miami Beach.

1

Loretta Oh, it's so beautiful here, George!

George Yeah, I'd like to live here someday.

Loretta Oh, I don't know. I love the city — the neighborhood, all the excitement. . .

George Excitement?! Is working twelve hours a day, seven days a week exciting? And the cold weather and the dirty snow? . . . Give me this beautiful sunshine any day!

Loretta Well, *I* like New York.

George Think of it, Loretta. . . . We could move here and open another little coffee shop — "Arno's South" — open from ten o'clock to one o'clock, three or four days a week. Oh, what a life!

Loretta What time is it now?

George It's a little after ten. Hmm . . . Nick is probably at the coffee shop right now, drinking his morning cup of coffee and talking to Jeff. And . . .

Loretta George, don't think about work. We're on vacation! Here, put on some more suntan lotion.

George Nah, I don't need any more.

Loretta You're going to get a terrible sunburn. This Florida sun is hot!

George Hey, that guy looks terrific. I think I'll get up and run with him. I need a little exercise.

Loretta Now don't do too much, George. You're not twenty years old.

George Don't worry, Loretta. I know what I'm doing. I'm just a little out of shape. I'll take it easy.

2. Figure it out

True, false, **or** *it doesn't say*?

1. The suntan lotion is going to give George a sunburn.
2. George is thinking about the coffee shop in New York.
3. Loretta likes to exercise.
4. George would like to move to Florida.
5. Loretta likes New York.
6. Loretta likes the snow.

▣ 3. Listen in

George talks to the runner.
Read the questions below.
Then listen to the conversation
and answer the questions.

1. How old is the runner?
2. How does he get to work?

▣ 4. How to say it

Listen to the conversation.

A How do you get to work?

B I drive. How do you get to
work?

A I take the train.

5. Your turn

Donna is listening to her cassette player when
Rob comes up and starts talking. What do you
think he's saying? Act out the conversation.

Rob _____
Donna Oh, hi.
Rob _____
Donna Yeah, it's a great day.
Rob _____
Donna Oh, I'm listening to a new rock group
called Fishbone. Do you like rock music?
Rob _____
Donna Well, this group is fantastic. Would you
like to listen to them?
Rob _____ (*Puts on headset.*)
Donna What's your opinion?
Rob _____
Donna What about rap music? Do you like that?
Rob _____
Donna Me either.

30.

Hotel Flamingo GARDENS

To help us give you the best service, the Flamingo Gardens Hotel would like the following information. Please take a minute to answer these questions.

1. **What is the purpose of your trip to Miami?**
   a. Vacation
   b. Business
   c. Other _____

2. **How did you travel here?**
   a. Plane
   b. Private Car
   c. Train
   d. Boat/ship

3. **How did you learn about the Flamingo Gardens Hotel?**
   a. Magazine Ad
   b. Newspaper Ad
   c. Travel Agent
   d. Other _____

4. **How would you grade your room for:**

   APPEARANCE   COMFORT
   a. Excellent a. Excellent
   b. Good   b. Good
   c. Fair   c. Fair
   d. Poor   d. Poor

5. **How would you grade the restaurant for:**

   FOOD QUALITY SERVICE
   a. Excellent a. Excellent
   b. Good   b. Good
   c. Fair   c. Fair
   d. Poor   d. Poor

6. **How would you grade the hotel staff for:**

   COURTESY   EFFICIENCY
   a. Excellent a. Excellent
   b. Good   b. Good
   c. Fair   c. Fair
   d. Poor   d. Poor

Today's Date _____   Room _____
Name _____
Address _____
_____
Telephone _____

---

1. **What's the purpose of the Flamingo Gardens Hotel Guest Survey? Scan the survey and choose the correct answer.**

   1. The hotel wants to improve its services.
   2. The hotel wants to make a list of its guests' names and addresses.

2. **Imagine you and your partner are guests at this hotel. Use the information below to complete the survey.**

   1. You came to Miami for a vacation on the beach.
   2. You arrived on flight 21 from your country.
   3. Your travel agent, IntraTours, chose the hotel.
   4. The room is beautiful, but it is on the second floor and you can hear the traffic all night long.
   5. You had lunch in the hotel restaurant. The food was pretty good and the service was fast.
   6. The hotel staff was very courteous and efficient.

PREVIEW

FUNCTIONS/THEMES	LANGUAGE	FORMS
Make a request	Could you open the window? Could you answer it for me?	*Could you . . . ?* Pronouns as objects of prepositions
Talk about the present	What do you do? What are you doing?	Simple present vs. present continuous
Say how you're doing Ask about an acquaintance Send greetings	I'm doing just great. How's Betsy doing? Say hi to her for me.	
Invite someone informally	I've got two tickets for the baseball game. Do you want to go?	*Have got*
Invite someone formally	Would you like to join us? I'd like to, but I can't. I have to work on Saturday.	*Have to* and *have got to*
Invite a friend to a party	When is it? In December. / On Sunday. / At five o'clock.	Prepositions *in, on,* and *at*

Preview the conversations.

We're going to go to a baseball game on Saturday. Would you like to join us?

I'd like to, but I can't. I have to take my car to the garage on Saturday.

We're going out after work. Do you want to come?

I'm sorry, I can't.

Here are two ways to invite someone. Both are appropriate for informal situations. Which one is also appropriate for formal situations?

Notice how these people refuse invitations. Which way is more polite? Why?

31. Would you like to join us?

 Some people are making plans to go to a baseball game.

A

Paula We're going to a baseball game on Saturday and we've got an extra ticket. Would you like to join us?

Jim Oh, I'd like to, but I can't. I have to take my car to the garage on Saturday. But thanks for inviting me.

Bob Are you sure? Rachel's going to go too.

Jim Oh, how's Rachel doing?

Paula She's doing fine. She loves her new job.

Jim Well, I really can't go, but say hi to her for me, O.K.?

Bob O.K. We will.

B

Bob Hey, Jack! Paula and I have an extra ticket to the baseball game. Do you want to go?

Jack That sounds great. When is it?

Bob Saturday at two.

Jack Oh, I'd really like to, but I have to work this Saturday.

Bob Oh, that's too bad. Well, maybe some other time.

C

Paula So, what are we going to do with that extra ticket?

Bob I don't know. Could you call Rachel after work? Maybe she knows someone who wants to go.

Paula O.K.

Mrs. Walters Hello?
Paula Hello, Mrs. Walters. This is Paula.
Is Rachel there?
Mrs. Walters She's eating dinner right
now, Paula. Could you call her back
in about half an hour?
Paula Sure.

Rachel Hello?
Paula Hi, Rachel. This is Paula.
Rachel Hi. How are you doing?
Paula Pretty good. I saw Jim today. He
says hello.
Rachel Oh, really? How's he doing?
Paula Oh, he's fine. Listen, we've still
got one ticket for the baseball game.
That's why I'm calling. Do you know
anyone who wants it?
Rachel Oh, Paula, I forgot to tell you. I
can't go either. Mom's having a
birthday party for my sister Saturday,
and I have to help.

Figure it out

**1. Listen to the conversations. Then answer the
questions.**

1. How many tickets do Paula and Bob have?
2. Who's going to go to the baseball game?

**2. Listen again and say *true*, *false*, or *it doesn't
say*.**

1. Something is wrong with Jim's car.
2. Rachel is Jim's girlfriend.
3. Rachel hates her new job.
4. Jack has to work every Saturday.
5. Paula calls Rachel about the extra ticket.
6. Rachel's birthday is Saturday.

3. Find another way to say it.

1. Would you like to go with us?
2. We have an extra ticket.
3. She's fine.
4. On Saturday at two o'clock.
5. Is Rachel at home?
6. How are you?

32. Could you call him for me?

MAKE A REQUEST • COULD YOU . . . ?

1 ▶ **What are they saying? Complete the requests with the sentences in the box.**
▶ **Listen to check your work.**

> Could you answer it for me?
> Could you close the door?
> Could you open the window?
> Could you help me with them?

▶ **Work with a partner. Make your own requests.**

My phone's ringing. _____

It's noisy in the hall. _____

These books are too heavy. _____

It's too hot in here. _____

PRONOUNS AS OBJECTS OF PREPOSITIONS

2 ▶ **Complete the conversation with object pronouns.**
▶ **Listen to check your work.**

Lawyer Mr. and Mrs. Walters and I are going to have lunch today. Do you want to come with _____ ?
Assistant Thanks, but I can't. I have to meet my son for lunch.
Lawyer Oh, that's nice. Say hi to _____ for _____ .
Assistant I will. What time are you going to meet the Walters?
Lawyer Good question! Could you call _____ for _____ and find out?
Assistant Sure.

Pronouns as objects of prepositions	
Could you call him for	me?
	us?
	him?
	her?
	them?

CALL SOMEONE • MAKE A REQUEST

3 ▶ **Listen to the conversation.**
▶ **Look at each picture and act out similar conversations with a partner.**

A Hello. Is Kenji there?
B He's eating dinner right now. Could you call him back in an hour?
A Sure. Thanks.

> Could you call back . . . ?
>
> | in half an hour | at about nine |
> | in ten minutes | before eleven |
> | at ten thirty | after seven |

Kenji

Julia

Alan

taking a shower

33. How's she doing?

TALK ABOUT THE PRESENT • SIMPLE PRESENT VS. PRESENT CONTINUOUS

1 ▶ **Study the frame.**

Simple present vs. present continuous
What **do** you **do**?   I **teach** English.
Do you **work** every day?   I **don't work** on Sundays.
What **are** you **doing**?   I**'m teaching** a class right now.
Are you **working** now?   I**'m not working** today.

2 ▶ **Complete the conversations with the verbs in parentheses.**
   ▶ **Listen to check your work.**

1. **A** Hello?
   B Hi, Tom. What _____ (do)?
   A Right now? _____ (read) a book. How about you? _____ (cook) dinner?
   B No. _____ (not cook) on Saturdays and Sundays. _____ (go out) for dinner on the weekends.

2. **A** I called Jim, but he wasn't at home. _____ (work) at the store today?
   B No, _____ (work) on Sundays. He's in Los Angeles.
   A Oh, _____ (visit) his brother?
   B Yes. _____ (visit) him every Sunday.

SAY HOW YOU'RE DOING

3 ▶ **Listen to what these people say about themselves.**
   ▶ **Tell your classmates how you're doing.**

Betsy Hill

Daniel Belei

Maria Tosca

1. I'm doing fine. I'm working a lot these days. But I'm lucky, I don't work on weekends. I play tennis every weekend.

2. I'm doing just great. I'm not studying English now. I have a job. In fact, I work for the telephone company.

3. I'm doing pretty well, but my mother isn't feeling well these days. I live with her now, so I take care of her.

ASK ABOUT AN ACQUAINTANCE • SEND GREETINGS

4 ▶ **Two people are talking about Betsy, above. Complete this conversation with the sentences in the box.**
   ▶ **Listen to check your work.**

A I'm going to have dinner with Betsy tonight.
B _____
A She's doing fine. She's working a lot these days.
B _____
A No. In fact, she plays tennis every weekend.
B _____
A O.K. I will.

Does she work on weekends?
Oh, how's she doing?
Well, say hi to her for me, O.K.?

▶ **Imagine you are going to see Daniel or call Maria. Have similar conversations.**

34. I'd like to, but I can't.

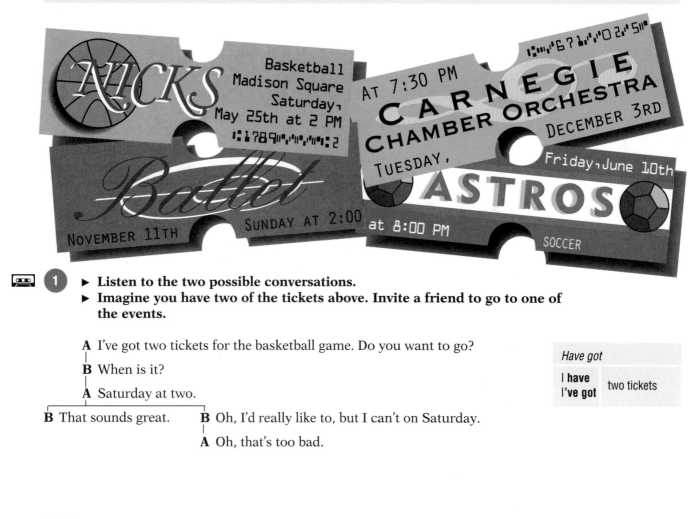

1 ▶ Listen to the two possible conversations.
▶ Imagine you have two of the tickets above. Invite a friend to go to one of the events.

A I've got two tickets for the basketball game. Do you want to go?

B When is it?

A Saturday at two.

B That sounds great.   **B** Oh, I'd really like to, but I can't on Saturday.

     A Oh, that's too bad.

Have got	
I **have**	
I**'ve got**	two tickets

INVITE SOMEONE FORMALLY • *HAVE TO* AND *HAVE GOT TO*

2 ▶ Listen to the two possible conversations.
▶ Work in groups of three. Invite someone you don't know very well to join you for coffee, lunch, or dinner.

A We're going out for dinner tonight. Would you like to join us?

B I'd love to. What time   **B** I'd like to, but I can't. I already have plans. I have to make
are you going?   dinner for my family tonight. But thanks for inviting me.

A At seven o'clock.   **A** Well, maybe some other time.

Have to and *have got to*	
I **have to**	work on Saturday.
I **'ve got to**	help my mother.
	go home right after work.
	work late.
	go to the dentist.
	take my car to the garage.

INVITE A FRIEND TO A PARTY • PREPOSITIONS *IN, ON,* AND *AT*

 3 ▶ Complete the telephone conversation with *in, on,* and *at.*
▶ Listen to check your work.

June Hello?
Fred June, it's Fred.
June Oh, hi, Fred.
Fred Listen, it's Alice's birthday next week. Would you like to come to her party?
June Sure. When is it?
Fred _____ Tuesday.
June Oh, we can't. Bill works late _____ Tuesdays.
Fred That's O.K. Come after work.
June Well, Bill isn't _____ home right now, but he'll be back _____ about an hour. Can I call you then?
Fred Sure.
June By the way, what time _____ Tuesday?
Fred _____ about eight o'clock.
June O.K. I'll check with Bill.

4 ▶ Study the frame.

In, on, and *at*

When is it?	In	December. two days.
	On	Sunday.
	At	five o'clock.

5 ▶ Listen to these conversations. Which of these people are coming to Alice's party?

GUEST LIST

	Yes	No
June	✓	
Bill		
Alex		
Ellen		
Steve		
Kim		

6 ▶ You just received this invitation to a party from your friend Teresa. Invite a friend to go with you.

A My friend Teresa is having a party. Do you want to go?
B Sure. When is it? . . .

I'm having a party and you're invited

Who: Teresa Gomez
Where: 245 Beacon St., Apt.3, Boston
When: Saturday, April 14th
What time: 8:30 p.m.
Bring a friend!

Would you like to come to my party?
I'd love to.
I _____ too.

Unit 6 **B 63**

35. Invite Jeff to come along.

Christine Pappas and her friends are talking after school.

1

Joe Hey, Chris . . . we're going out for pizza tonight. You want to come along?

Chris Gee, I'd really like to, but I have to ask my parents.

Joe Well, call me when you get home.

Katy Hey, look over there. Who's that with Ms. Rogers?

Chris I don't know, but I see them together a lot.

Joe He's probably her boyfriend.

Chris Shh! She'll hear you!

Joe Hey, Chris, there's Jeff.

Chris Hmm . . . maybe he'd like to come with us tonight.

Katy Yeah, Chris, invite Jeff to come along.

Chris *You* invite him, Katy. You know him better.

Katy O.K. Oh, wait — he can't come anyway. He has to work.

Chris Oh, that's right. He works on Wednesdays . . . Hey, does anyone know what time it is?

Katy Yeah, it's almost three thirty.

Chris Oh, it's late. I've got to get home. Well, maybe I'll see you later.

Joe Bye, Chris. Don't forget to call!

2. Figure it out

True, false, or it doesn't say?

1. Joe and Katy invite Chris for pizza. *True.*
2. Chris already has plans.
3. Joe thinks the man with Ms. Rogers is her boyfriend.
4. Jeff works after school on Wednesdays.
5. Ms. Rogers teaches English.
6. Katy invites Jeff to join them for pizza.
7. Chris is in a hurry to get home.

📼 3. Listen in

Liz Rogers' friend Paul meets her at school. He tells her that their friends the Lees have invited them to dinner. Read the statements below. Then listen to the conversation and choose *a* or *b*.

1. The Lees invite Liz and Paul to dinner _____ .
   a. this Sunday
   b. next Sunday

2. Liz _____ have dinner with the Lees.
   a. can
   b. can't

📼 4. How to say it

Listen to the conversation.

A Do you <u>want to</u> go to   [wanə]
a movie after work?

B Oh, I'd really <u>like to</u>   [layktə]
go, but I can't. I <u>have to</u>   [hæftə]
make dinner for my family.

5. Your turn

It's Wednesday. Jeff's friend Bill invites him to play basketball, but Jeff has to work. Act out the conversation.

Bill   _____

Jeff I'd really like to, but I can't. I have to work.

Bill   _____

Jeff Oh, I work at Arno's Coffee Shop.

Bill   _____

Jeff No, I don't work every day. Just Wednesdays, Fridays, and Saturdays.

Bill   _____

Jeff Tomorrow? Sure. That sounds good.

Bill   _____

Jeff O.K. Bye.

36.

Did You Know?

Here are some things you may or may not know about people in the United States and the way they live. Some of them may surprise you.

- The U.S. population is approximately 250 million.
- Between 1980 and 1990, forty percent of the population increase in the U.S. was due to immigration.
- Most of today's immigrants are from Mexico, the Philippines and China.
- California has a larger population than either Canada or Australia.
- The average annual income is about $25,000 although 7% of the population is unemployed.
- About twenty percent of the population moves every year.
- On the average, a person in the U.S. changes jobs about every four years.
- There are an estimated 250,000 homeless people in the cities and towns of the U.S.
- The average cost of college tuition per year is $11,269 at a private university and $4,711 at a public university.
- Approximately twenty-three percent of American women and thirty percent of American men never marry.
- On the average, people spend only 20 minutes eating dinner.
- Americans eat an average of 16 lbs. of ice cream every year.

Answer the questions with *true, false,* or *it doesn't say*.

1. People in the U.S. move a lot.
2. Everyone has a job in the U.S.
3. People change their jobs every year.
4. Everyone has a home.
5. A college education is usually free.
6. The population of California is larger than the population of Australia.
7. Most immigrants to the U.S. come from Europe.
8. Everyone in the U.S. gets married.
9. People in the U.S. like long dinners.
10. People usually eat ice cream at dinner.

PREVIEW

FUNCTIONS/THEMES	LANGUAGE	FORMS
Ask about something you found	I found this pen. Is it yours?	Possessive adjectives and pronouns
Talk about possessions	This is my pen.	
Listen to opinions about jobs Give opinions about jobs	Elena is a teacher. She likes it a lot. A plumber's job is hard work, but the pay is good.	
Ask where to buy something Give directions Offer to do a favor	Where can you get some aspirin? There's a drugstore on Ridge Road. Can I get you anything?	Impersonal pronoun *you*
Compare yourself to someone Talk about eating habits	I'm like Manolo. I always have a big lunch around 2:00 P.M.	Frequency adverbs

Preview the conversations.

These two men live and work in the United States. Like most Americans, they eat three meals a day — breakfast, lunch, and dinner. Sometimes they have coffee or eat snacks between meals.

How many meals do you usually eat every day? Do you ever get hungry between meals? What do you eat or drink then?

37. First day on the job?

Pete Hall is starting a new job.

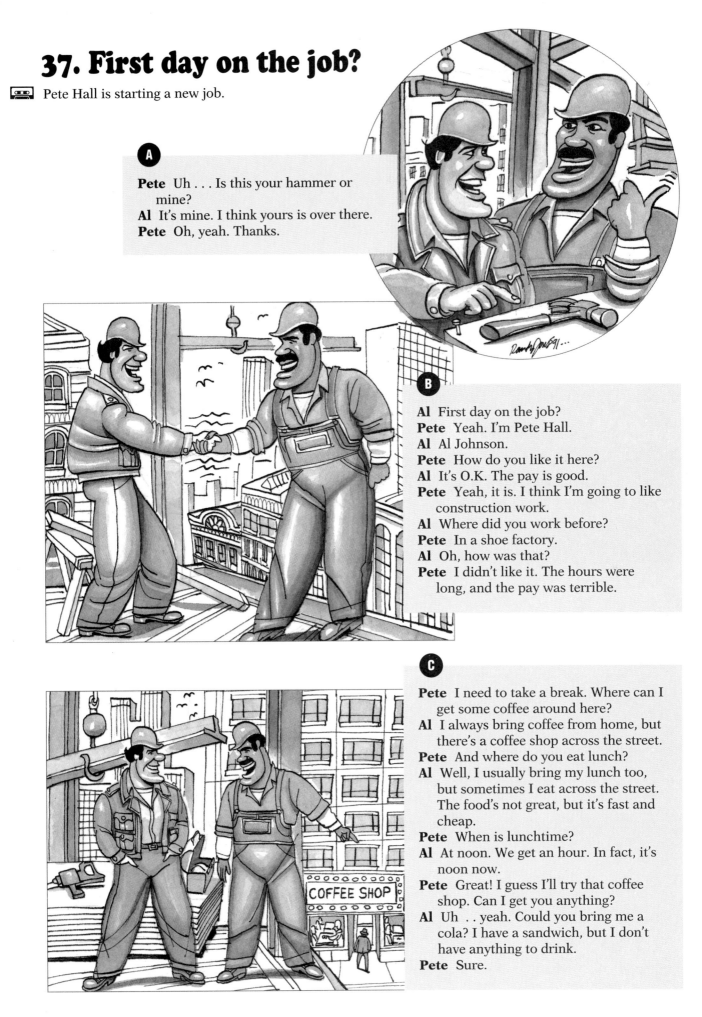

A

Pete Uh . . . Is this your hammer or mine?
Al It's mine. I think yours is over there.
Pete Oh, yeah. Thanks.

B

Al First day on the job?
Pete Yeah. I'm Pete Hall.
Al Al Johnson.
Pete How do you like it here?
Al It's O.K. The pay is good.
Pete Yeah, it is. I think I'm going to like construction work.
Al Where did you work before?
Pete In a shoe factory.
Al Oh, how was that?
Pete I didn't like it. The hours were long, and the pay was terrible.

C

Pete I need to take a break. Where can I get some coffee around here?
Al I always bring coffee from home, but there's a coffee shop across the street.
Pete And where do you eat lunch?
Al Well, I usually bring my lunch too, but sometimes I eat across the street. The food's not great, but it's fast and cheap.
Pete When is lunchtime?
Al At noon. We get an hour. In fact, it's noon now.
Pete Great! I guess I'll try that coffee shop. Can I get you anything?
Al Uh . . yeah. Could you bring me a cola? I have a sandwich, but I don't have anything to drink.
Pete Sure.

COFFEE SHOP

Waitress What would you like?
Pete A hamburger and french fries.
Waitress To stay or to go?
Pete To go, please.
Waitress Something to drink?
Pete Yeah. How's your coffee?
Waitress Uh . . . Well, I never drink it!
Pete Two colas then.
Waitress Anything else?
Pete No, that's all. Thanks.

Figure it out

1. Listen to the conversation and choose *a*, *b*, or *c*.

1. a. One of the men is going to have a hamburger for lunch.
   b. Both of the men are going to have hamburgers for lunch.
2. a. One of the men is going to have a cola with his lunch.
   b. Both of the men are going to have colas with their lunch.

2. Listen again. Say *true*, *false*, or *it doesn't say*.

1. Pete lost his hammer. *False.*
2. It's Pete's first day at work.
3. Pete would like a cup of coffee.
4. The waitress likes the food at the coffee shop.
5. Al always brings coffee from home.
6. Pete is going to eat his lunch in the coffee shop.

3. Find another way to say it.

1. It's my hammer. *It's mine.*
2. Do you want anything?
3. Do you want to eat here in the coffee shop or not?
4. Is your coffee good or bad?
5. What do you think of this job?
6. It's not expensive.

38. Is this yours?

  1 ▶ **Listen to the conversation.**
▶ **Have similar conversations with your classmates.**

A I found this pen. Is it yours?
B No. Mine is right here. Maybe it's his (hers).
A Excuse me, is this pen yours?
C Yes, it is. Thanks a lot.

2 ▶ **Imagine you found one of the items in the box. Find the owner.**

Some personal possessions	
pen	copy of *Spectrum*
keys	gloves
notebook	umbrella
wallet	coat

TALK ABOUT POSSESSIONS • POSSESSIVE ADJECTIVES AND PRONOUNS

3 ▶ **Study the frames.**

Possessive adjectives	
This is	**my pen.** **your pen.** **his pen.** **her pen.** **our pen.** **their pen.**

Possessive pronouns	
This pen is	**mine.** **yours.** **his.** **hers.** **ours.** **theirs.**

Possessive adjectives and pronouns have one form. They do not change for plural nouns.

This is **my** pen.   This pen is **mine**.
These are **my** pens. These pens are **mine**.

---

  4 ▶ **Complete the conversations with possessive pronouns.**
▶ **Listen to check your answers.**

Is this your earring?

Yes. _____ .

Is this your English book?

No. _____ .
Your name is in it.

Is this your calculator?

No. I think _____ .

Is this your car?

Yes. _____ .
We're sorry.

Is this your address book?

No. I think _____ .

Are these your shoes?

No. I think _____ .

39. What do you do?

 1 ▶ **Listen to a radio interview with Elena Cardenas from Santiago, Chile, and Jim Wilson from Chicago, Illinois. Then answer the questions below.**

1. What does Elena do? Does she like her job?
2. What does Jim do? Does he like his job?

2 ▶ **What's your opinion of these professions? Complete the survey.**

Which of these sentences are true about the professions below?	It's interesting.	It's boring.	It's easy.	It's hard work.	The pay is good.	The pay is terrible.	The hours are long.	It's dangerous.	It's exciting.
plumber									
actor/actress									
pilot									
artist									
lawyer									
teacher									
police officer									
cook									
computer programmer									
dentist									

▶ **Share your opinions about jobs.**

A What do you think about a plumber's job?
B Well, it's hard work, but the pay is good.

 3 ▶ **Listen to the conversation.**
   ▶ **Practice the conversation with a partner.**

A What do you do?
B I'm a pilot.
A Oh, how do you like it?
B Well, I like it a lot, but it's hard work. How about you? What do you do?
A I'm a computer programmer.
B How do you like your job?
A Not too much, actually. The pay is good, but it's boring.

4 ▶ **Talk with your classmates.**

Now talk about your own job or imagine you have one of the jobs in exercise 2. Tell your classmates how you like it.

How do you like your job?	
It's great. I like it a lot.	😊
It's O.K. It's not too bad.	😐
Not too much. I don't like it at all.	☹️

40. Where can I get some coffee?

ASK WHERE TO BUY SOMETHING • IMPERSONAL PRONOUN *YOU*

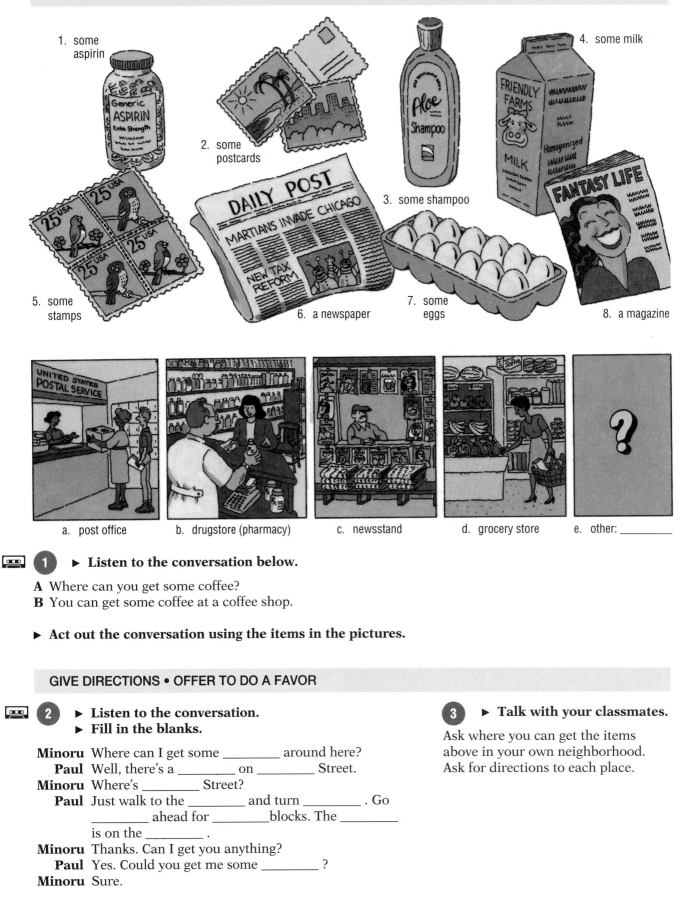

1. some aspirin
2. some postcards
3. some shampoo
4. some milk
5. some stamps
6. a newspaper
7. some eggs
8. a magazine

a. post office
b. drugstore (pharmacy)
c. newsstand
d. grocery store
e. other: _____

1 ▶ **Listen to the conversation below.**

A Where can you get some coffee?
B You can get some coffee at a coffee shop.

▶ **Act out the conversation using the items in the pictures.**

GIVE DIRECTIONS • OFFER TO DO A FAVOR

2 ▶ **Listen to the conversation.**
▶ **Fill in the blanks.**

Minoru Where can I get some _____ around here?
Paul Well, there's a _____ on _____ Street.
Minoru Where's _____ Street?
Paul Just walk to the _____ and turn _____ . Go _____ ahead for _____ blocks. The _____ is on the _____ .
Minoru Thanks. Can I get you anything?
Paul Yes. Could you get me some _____ ?
Minoru Sure.

3 ▶ **Talk with your classmates.**

Ask where you can get the items above in your own neighborhood. Ask for directions to each place.

41. I always go out to lunch.

COMPARE YOURSELF TO SOMEONE

 1 ▶ Read along as you listen to what these people say about eating lunch.

What do you usually do for lunch?

Margarida Silva
Translator
Porto Alegre,
Brazil

I always go out
for lunch — usually around 3:00.
I never go home.

Manolo Gonzalez
Store manager
Guadalajara,
Mexico
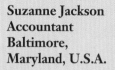

I always go home for
lunch. I usually have a very big
lunch around 2:00.

Suzanne Jackson
Accountant
Baltimore,
Maryland, U.S.A.

I usually eat around
12:30. I often take my lunch to
work. Restaurants are so
expensive.

2 ▶ **Talk to your classmates. Compare yourself to the people above.**

A I'm like Manolo. I always have a big lunch around 2:00.
B I'm like Suzanne. I usually eat early, at about 12:00 or 12:30 — but I don't take my lunch to work.

TALK ABOUT EATING HABITS • FREQUENCY ADVERBS

3 ▶ **Study the frame.**

Frequency adverbs

Do you	**always** **usually** **often**	eat at two o'clock?	I	**always** **usually** **often**	eat at two o'clock.	100% ↓
Are you	**sometimes** **ever**	hungry at noon?	I'm	**sometimes** **never**	hungry at noon.	0%

 4 ▶ **Listen to the conversation below.**
▶ **Practice the conversation with a partner.**

A Do you ever go home for lunch?
B No. I always eat at a restaurant near work. I only
have a half hour for lunch.
A What do you eat?
B I usually have a sandwich.

5 ▶ **Interview your classmates.**

Find out what three classmates usually do for
lunch.

 6 ▶ **Listen to the conversation.**
▶ **Order your own lunch. Work in pairs and act out the conversation.**

A What would you like?
B A hamburger and french fries.
A Is that to stay or to go?
B To go, please.
A Something to drink?
B A cup of coffee.
A Anything else?
B No, that's all, thanks.

chicken
sandwich

hamburger

orange juice   cola   tea   coffee

french fries

cheeseburger

42. Is your postcard from the Arnos?

George and Loretta are in their hotel room.

View of Miami Beach, Miami, Florida

Dear Nick and Stella,
Greetings from Miami Beach!

See you soon!

Love,
Loretta and George

P.S. We miss you!

Mr. and Mrs. N. Pappas
27 Willow Street
Brooklyn, NY 11201

1. Listen in

Back in their hotel room, George and Loretta are talking while Loretta writes some postcards. Read the statements below. Then listen to the conversation and say *true* or *false*.

1. Loretta doesn't want to go to a restaurant.
2. George has a sunburn.

2. Your turn

Complete the postcard for Loretta. Include this information.

1. Loretta tells Nick and Stella they're having a wonderful time.
2. She tells them the weather in Miami is beautiful.
3. She asks about the weather in New York.
4. She sends greetings to Christine.

Meanwhile, back on Willow Street . . .

3

John Excuse me, miss — is this yours?
Carolyn Oh . . . yes, it is. Thanks.
John Wait a minute. . . . I got a postcard just like it. Is yours from the Arnos?
Carolyn (*Surprised*) Why, yes! Do you know them?
John Well, they're my neighbors.
Carolyn Really? They're mine too.

4

John Oh, yeah? Where do you live?
Carolyn In that building over there — number 3.
John Me too. I live in 1B.
Carolyn No kidding! I live right above you — in 2B.
John Oh, then you must be Carolyn Laval.
Carolyn *Du*val. And you're . . . don't tell me . . . J. Pierce.
John Right! The "J" is for John.

5

Carolyn What do you play?
John Huh? Oh, you mean this. . . . I play the saxophone.
Carolyn Really? Do you play any jazz?
John Sure. I love jazz.
Carolyn I do too. I play the string bass.

6. Figure it out

***True, false,* or *it doesn't say*?**

1. Carolyn got a card from the Arnos and John did too. *True.*
2. Carolyn lives at 3 Willow Street and John does too.
3. Carolyn likes jazz and John does too.
4. Carolyn plays the string bass and John does too.
5. Carolyn plays well and John does too.

7. Your turn

How do you think Carolyn and John's conversation ends? Act out the conversation, finishing John's part.

Carolyn Are you a professional musician?
John _____
Carolyn I'm not either. I'm an actress.
John _____
Carolyn I like it a lot — when I'm working! Say, would you like to go out for coffee?
John _____

8. How to say it

Listen to the conversation.

A <u>Where do you</u> work?   [werdəyuw]
B At the *Press*.
A <u>Where did you</u> work before? [werdɪdʒuw]
B At the *Record*.

43.

World Note

To begin their day, many people around the world wake up and have a cup of coffee or tea. But as for what people eat in the morning the variety is almost as great as the number of countries. We were not able to include all of the responses we received, but we think you'll find these examples interesting.

Olivier Barre
Nancy, France

My favorite thing for breakfast is croissants. Croissants are a kind of bread and in my family we always have them on Sundays. We get them fresh from the bakery down the street. I have mine with a cup of hot chocolate. My parents have coffee.

Kamala Natarajan
Madras, India

Besides coffee, we have several things for breakfast. For example, there is *idli*, a kind of warm rice cake, and *dosa*, a thin pancake made with rice and lentils. Also, there is something called *upma* which is ground wheat cooked with spices. We eat all this with *chutney*, a kind of jam made from coconut or mangoes.

Costa Vassos
Salonika, Greece

A simple breakfast of butter and honey on fresh bread is what my family eats. We also have coffee — good strong Greek coffee. Sometimes we eat yogurt and we put honey in that too.

Shirley Luck
Leeds, England

I like a big breakfast in the morning — fried eggs and bacon, or maybe porridge, kippers, and toast. Porridge is boiled cereal and kippers are a type of smoked fish. And, of course, I always have a pot of good breakfast tea.

Cesar Mendoza
Monterrey, Mexico

My favorite breakfast is *huevos rancheros*. *Huevos rancheros* are fried eggs served with hot sauce on top of fried beans and a tortilla. When I have them for breakfast, I don't need any lunch.

Yoko Higuchi
Tokyo, Japan

When I have time, I have a bowl of hot rice with a raw egg and some dried fish. Sometimes, just coffee and toast is good too. In any case, I usually don't eat much for breakfast.

Read the article. Then answer *true, false,* or *it doesn't say.*

1. *Huevos rancheros* is a big breakfast for Cesar Mendoza.
2. Olivier Barre lives near a bakery.
3. Yoko Higuchi doesn't always have time for a breakfast of rice, egg, and fish.
4. Costa Vassos has two cups of Greek coffee with his breakfast.
5. Shirley Luck has coffee with her breakfast.
6. Kamala Natarajan eats *chutney* with every meal.

Review of Units 5-7

1 ▶ Jim Eldred and Tom Kio go to college in San Francisco. Fill in the blanks with prepositions.
▶ Act out the conversation with a partner.

Tom How was your day?

Jim Not too good. I went _____ the library, but I was bored and I left _____ noon.

Tom Oh, I was _____ the library, too. In fact, I found this book there. Is it yours?

Jim No, I think it's Ann Lorca's book.

Tom Do you think she's _____ home now?

Jim No, she's _____ class, but she'll be back _____ an hour.

Tom Well, could you give her the book _____ me?

Jim Sure. I'm going to have lunch _____ her _____ Sunday.

Tom Great.

2 ▶ Imagine you found something. Try to find the owner. Use the items in the pictures or other items.

A I found this book in the library. Is it yours?
B Yes, it's mine. Thanks.

A I found these glasses on the table. Are they yours?
B No, they're not mine. I think they're Ann's.

3 ▶ It's Friday night and Jim Eldred and Ann Lorca are talking. Listen and check the kinds of food they like.

	Jim	Ann
Seafood		
French food		
Italian food		
Indian food		
Chinese food		
Japanese food		
Mexican food		
Fast food		

4 ▶ Make comments about Jim and Ann.

A Jim likes seafood, but Ann doesn't.
B Jim doesn't like French food and Ann doesn't either.

5 ▶ Interview your classmates.

Make a chart like the one above. Ask three classmates about the foods they like.

6 ▶ **Tom wants to go out to dinner with his friend Gina. Fill in the blanks with *the* where necessary.**

Tom Do you like _____ hamburgers?

Gina Sure. Why?

Tom Well, there's a restaurant called Lulu's and _____ hamburgers there are excellent. Would you like to go tonight?

Gina I'd like to, but I can't. I have to babysit for _____ neighbors.

Tom Well, maybe some other time.

Gina O.K. Oh, by the way, I know you like _____ rock music. _____ music at the Underground Club is great. You really have to go!

Tom Yeah, I know. Maybe this weekend.

▶ **Act out the conversation with a partner. Use the ads on the right or your own information.**

Food	
Benny's	seafood
The Chateau	French cuisine
The New Moon	Chinese specialities
Lulu's	for the best hamburgers & hot dogs

Entertainment	
The Underground Club	new rock groups every night
Sally's	jazz at 9:00 P.M. and 11:00 P.M.
The Living Room	classical piano music every evening
Nashville	country music

7 ▶ **It's Saturday. Ann meets her friend Helene Garcia at the library. Complete Helene's part of the conversation.**

Ann I'm going to have lunch with Jim tomorrow. Would you like to join us?

Helene _____

Ann At about noon.

Helene _____

Ann Oh, that's too bad. Well, maybe some other time.

Helene _____

Ann By the way, I've got two tickets for the ballet next Saturday night. Do you want to go?

Helene _____

Ann Great! I'll meet you at the theater at ten to eight.

▶ **Invite your partner to join you for a meal and for the ballet or a concert.**

8 ▶ **Complete the conversation.**
▶ **Act out a similar conversation with a partner.**

Helene _____

Ann Oh, Jim's doing fine.

Helene _____

Ann No, he doesn't live here in San Francisco now. He moved to a small town in the country.

Helene _____

Ann He loves it. In his opinion, it's quiet and cheap.

Helene _____

Ann He takes the train. It takes him about forty-five minutes.

Helene _____

Ann O.K.

9 ▶ It's Sunday and Ann is waiting for Jim at Lulu's. A stranger begins talking to her. Complete Ann's part of the conversation with the sentences in the box

Man Beautiful day.
Ann _____
Man Do you live here in San Francisco?
Ann _____
Man Do you like it here?
Ann _____
Man Why?
Ann _____
Man What do you do for a living?
Ann _____
Man How do you like it?
Ann _____

I like it very much.
I'm a doctor.
Yes, I do.
The hours are long, but I like it very much.
Yes, it is.
Because the city is beautiful. There are interesting old houses and wonderful parks.

▶ Work with a partner. Say why you like the place where you live. Your partner will agree or disagree.

10 ▶ You are at Lulu's restaurant. Look at the menu and order lunch. Your partner will write down your order.

LULU'S Restaurant

SANDWICHES
hamburger	$3.95
cheeseburger	$4.95
with lettuce and tomato	$1.00 extra
hot dog	$2.75
chicken sandwich	$3.50
steak sandwich	$5.95
fish sandwich	$4.75

SIDE ORDERS
french fries	$1.10
potato salad	$1.10

DRINKS
	small	large
soda		
cola, diet cola, orange	.65	.95
coffee, tea	.65	
milk	.45	

11A ▶ Student A follows the instructions below. Student B follows the instructions on page B80.

Student A Imagine you received this invitation to a party. Invite your partner and answer his or her questions. Then ask appropriate questions and accept or decline your partner's invitation.

I'm having a party and you're invited

Who: *Ann Lorca*
Where: *83 Hernandez Avenue, San Francisco, CA*
When: *Friday, November 10th*
What time: *8:00 p.m.*

Bring a friend!

▶ **Student B follows the instructions below.**

Student A follows the instruction on p. B79.

Student B Ask appropriate questions and accept or decline your partner's invitation. Then imagine you received this invitation to a picnic. Invite your partner and answer his or her questions.

Hi—

I'm having a picnic on Saturday afternoon July 18th at 2:00. Everyone is meeting in Golden Gate Park near the Japanese Tea Garden. Then we'll look for a good place for the picnic.

Please bring a friend and join us. I hope to see you on Saturday.

Tom Kio

P.S. I'll bring all the food and drinks.

12 ▶ **You are preparing for a birthday party on Friday and you still need several things from the store. Ask your classmates where you can get these things in your neighborhood.**

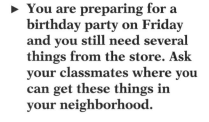

some balloons

some paper napkins

some soda

some plastic forks

some paper plates

a cake

some paper cups

13 ▶ **Read the article about Tom and answer the questions.**
▶ **Ask your partner similar questions.**

1. Does Tom work hard?
2. Does he enjoy it?
3. Where does he usually eat lunch?
4. Does Tom play any sports? What sport(s)?
5. When does he play?
6. What does he do in the evenings?
7. What does he often do on weekends?

PROFILE: *Tom Kio*

Tom Kio is a very busy man. He's a student in the architecture department at San Francisco State University and he has a part-time job at Benning Design Associates. Tom works hard, but he enjoys what he does. He usually arrives at his office at eight o'clock in the morning and works until one. He always eats lunch at his desk at work. Then he leaves for the university.

Tom is busy in the evening , too. He usually studies for several hours every night. On Mondays and Wednesdays, however, he always plays tennis — he really loves sports. When he has time, he sometimes goes out for dinner or to a movie with friends.

On the weekends, Tom often invites 15 or 20 friends to join him for a picnic in the park. His favorite activity at a picnic — playing baseball.

VOCABULARY LIST

The list includes both productive and receptive words introduced in Student Book 1B. Productive words are those which students use actively in interaction exercises. Receptive words are those which appear only in opening conversations, comprehension dialogues, readings, and instructions, and which students need only understand. The R appears after each receptive word. Page numbers indicate the first appearance of a word. In the case of productive words, the page indicated is where the word is first used productively. These words generally have been introduced receptively in previous units. This list does not include countries, languages, or nationalities. These are given in the supplementary vocabulary on pages B85–86. The following abbreviations are used to indicate parts of speech: V = verb, N = noun, ADJ = adjective, ADV = adverb, PR = pronoun, INTERJ = interjection, 3RD PERS SING = third person singular, PL = plural.

A

able 76 R
about (ADV) (about nine) 60
academy 42 R
accept (V) 79 R
across 32 R
actor 71
actress 71
actually 71
address book 70
adult 10 R
adventure 18
after 12 R
after 17
agent 22 R
aggressive 10 R
ago 32 R
ahead (go ahead) 72 R
alive 42 R
all over 11 R
all right 24 R
all the time 10 R
almost 21 R
along 64 R
already 62 R
always 73
ankle 42 R
answer (V) 60
anyone 42 R
anything 24 R
anyway (ADV) 20 R
appearance 56 R
apple 29
appointment 2 R
approval 42 R
approximately 66 R
architecture 11 R
around (ADV) (around three) 73
arrange (V) 42 R
art 16
artist 71
as . . . as 42 R
as for 76 R
as well as 22 R
aspirin 72
assistant 8 R

at (+time) 2 R
at home 7
at least 21 R
average 10 R
award 42 R
away 41 R
awful 19

B

babysit (V) 78 R
back 13 R
bacon 76 R
bad 27
bag (of) 28
bakery 76 R
ball (=dance) 22 R
ballet 36
balloon 80
banana 28
baseball 57 R
based (on) 42 R
basic 26 R
basketball 65
bass (string bass) 75 R
bathing suit 30 R
bean (fried beans) 76 R
beautiful 4
became (past of become) 32 R
because 10 R
bed (go to bed) 35 R
bedroom 40 R
beef (ground beef) 29
before 60
behind 5
belong (to) (V) 22 R
belonging (N) 4 R
belt 4
besides 19
best-seller 42 R
better (comparative of good) 64 R
big 76 R
biggest (superlative of big) 32 R
bike (=bicycle) 50
bikini 21 R
black 4

blouse 4
blue 4
boat 56 R
boiled (ADJ) 76 R
boring 16
bought (past of buy) 22 R
bowl (of) 76 R
boyfriend 42 R
break (N) 68 R
briefcase 4
bright 8 R
broken (ADJ) 42 R
brown 4
built (past of build) 22 R
bus 50
but (PREP) 24 R
butter 76 R
by any chance 3 R
by the time 10 R

C

cafeteria 6
cake 80
calculator 70
calm (down) (V) 40 R
calmly 10 R
came (past of come) 21 R
can (V) 10 R
can't (=cannot) 21 R
cantaloupe 29
car 7
card (=postcard) 75 R
care (take care of) 61 R
carrot 27
carry (V) 32 R
case (in any case) 76 R
cassette player 55 R
category 18 R
celebrate (V) 22 R
celebration 22 R
cent 27
center 22 R
century 22 R
cereal 10 R
certain 80 R

chance (by any change) 3 R
change (V) 10 R
cheap 50 R
cheeseburger 73
chicken 28
chicken sandwich 73
child 10 R
chocolate 76 R
chop (pork chop) 29
chose (past of choose) 56 R
chutney 76 R
circle (V) 15 R
classic 18
classical 49 R
clean (ADJ) 8 R
clean (V) 38
close (V) 60
closed (ADJ) 51 R
closet 5
clothing 4 R
cloudy 15
club 13 R
coat 4
coconut 76 R
coffee table 5
cola 73
cold 15
college 77 R
colony 22 R
color 4
colorful 22 R
come along 64 R
come from 32 R
come on 12 R
comedy 18
comfort 56 R
comment (N) 77 R
commercial 8 R
commission 22 R
community 22 R
compliment (N and V) 1 R
computer programmer 71
concert 10 R
construction 68 R
contain (V) 26 R

SUPPLEMENTARY VOCABULARY

SOME COLORS

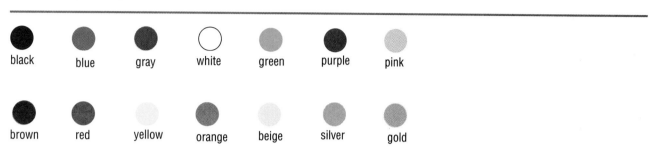

black blue gray white green purple pink

brown red yellow orange beige silver gold

SOME SPORTS

baseball	racquetball
basketball	rugby
cricket	sailing
fencing	skiing
football	soccer
hiking	swimming
horseback riding	tennis
ice hockey	track and field
ice skating	volleyball
mountain climbing	water skiing

WEIGHTS AND MEASURES

English System

Linear Measure

12 inches (in.)	=	1 foot (ft.)
3 feet	=	1 yard (yd.)
1760 yards	=	1 mile (mi.)
(5280 feet)		

Liquid Measure

16 fluid ounces (oz.)	=	1 pint (pt.)
2 pints	=	1 quart (qt.)
4 quarts	=	1 gallon (gal.)

Weight

16 ounces	=	1 pound (lb.)
1 ton	=	2000 pounds (U.S.)
	=	2240 pounds (Great Britain)

Metric and English Equivalents

Linear Measure

1 inch (in.)	=	2.54 centimeters (cm)
1 foot	=	30.48 centimeters
1 yard	=	0.9144 meters (m)
1 mile	=	1609.3 meters

Liquid Measure

1 quart	=	0.946 liters
1 gallon	=	13.78 liters

Weight

1 ounce	=	28.3 grams (g)
1 pound	=	0.45 kilograms (kg)
1 ton (U.S.)	=	907.18 kilograms
1 ton (Great Britain)	=	1,016 kilograms

SOME COUNTRIES AND NATIONALITIES

Country	Nationality	Country	Nationality
Algeria	Algerian	Korea	Korean
Argentina	Argentine	Laos	Laotian
Afghanistan	Afghan	Latvia	Latvian
Australia	Australian	Lebanon	Lebanese
Austria	Austrian	Lithuania	Lithuanian
Bolivia	Bolivian	Malaysia	Malaysian
Brazil	Brazilian	Mexico	Mexican
Bulgaria	Bulgarian	Mongolia	Mongolian
Canada	Canadian	Morocco	Moroccan
Chad	Chadian	Nepal	Nepalese
Chile	Chilean	Nicaragua	Nicaraguan
China	Chinese	Nigeria	Nigerian
Colombia	Colombian	Norway	Norwegian
Cost Rica	Costa Rican	Pakistan	Pakistani
Cuba	Cuban	Paraguay	Paraguayan
Czechoslovakia	Czech	Peru	Peruvian
Ecuador	Ecuadorian	Panama	Panamanian
Egypt	Egyptian	Poland	Polish
Estonia	Estonian	Portugal	Portuguese
Ethiopia	Ethiopian	Saudi Arabia	Saudi
Finland	Finnish	Spain	Spanish
France	French	Somalia	Somalian
Gambia	Gambian	Sweden	Swedish
Germany	German	Switzerland	Swiss
Guyana	Guyanese	Syria	Syrian
Ghana	Ghanan	Thailand	Thai
Greece	Greek	The Dominican Republic	Dominican
Guatemala	Guatemalan		
Haiti	Haitian	The Netherlands	Dutch
Honduras	Honduran	The Philippines	Filipino
Hungary	Hungarian	The United Kingdom	British
India	Indian	The United States of America	American
Indonesia	Indonesian		
Iran	Iranian	Tunisia	Tunisian
Iraq	Iraqi	Turkey	Turkish
Ireland	Irish	Venezuela	Venezuelan
Israel	Israeli	Vietnam	Vietnamese
Italy	Italian	Zaire	Zairian
Japan	Japanese	Zambia	Zambian
Jordan	Jordanian		
Kenya	Kenyan		
Kuwait	Kuwaiti		

SOME LANGUAGES

Arabic	French	Mandarin	Swahili
Bengali	German	Mongolian	Swedish
Cantonese	Greek	Nahuatl	Tagalog
Czech	Hausa	Norwegian	Tamil
Danish	Hebrew	Polish	Thai
Dutch	Hindi	Portuguese	Turkish
English	Hungarian	Quechua	Urdu
Estonian	Italian	Romanian	Vietnamese
Farsi	Japanese	Russian	Zulu
Finnish	Korean	Spanish	

P R O N U N C I A T I O N

STRESS AND INTONATION

Affirmative statement: I like old movies.

Yes–no question: Is this it?

Information question: What time is it?

PHONETIC SYMBOLS*

Consonants

[p]	pen, apple
[b]	bank, cabbage
[f]	far, after
[v]	very, have
[k]	coffee, like
[g]	good, again
[l]	letter, mile
[m]	many, name
[n]	never, money
[w]	water, away
[θ]	think, with
[ð]	the, mother
[s]	some, dress
[z]	zero, busy
[ʃ]	shoe, information
[ʒ]	pleasure, measure
[tʃ]	children, teach
[dʒ]	job, age
[r]	right, hurry
[y]	year, million
[h]	he, hat, who
[t]	ten, can't
[d]	dinner, idea

Vowels

[ɪ]	in, visit
[i]	meet, tea
[ɛ]	end, let, any
[æ]	ask, family
[a]	father, hot
[ɔ]	water, long
[ω]	could, put
[u]	you, room
[ə]	across, but
[ɚ]	her, work
[e]	wait, great
[o]	home, go
[aɪ]	dime, night
[ɔɪ]	toy, boy
[aω]	found, house

*[ə] and [ɚ] are used in this book, for both stressed and unstressed syllables. [y] is used instead of the International Phonetic Alphabet (IPA) [j].

ACKNOWLEDGMENTS

ILLUSTRATIONS

Storyline illustrations by Anna Veltfort: pages B8-9, B20-21, B30-31, B40-41, B54-55, B64-65, B74-75, pages B5 (bottom), B12-13, B70, B72, B77(top, bottom), B80; pages B1 (left), B2-3, B16, B43 (middle), B44 (top) by Chris Reed; pages B1(right), B2-3, B16, B43 (middle), B44 (top) by Jim Kinstrey; pages B4, B36 by Susan Tomlingson; page B5 (bottom) by Roberto de Vicq; page B6 by Ron Barrett; pages B7, B33, B34-35, B37, B39 by Ivor Parry; page B14 by Daisy de Puthod; pages B15, B17 (middle), B24-25, B47, B48-49 by Gene Myers; pages B23, B26, B27, B38, B45, B46 (top), B73, B77 (middle) by Don Martinetti; page B28 (watermelon) by David Riccardi; page B52 by Cathy Braffet; page B53 by Sylvio Redinger; pages B60, B62 (bottom) by Anne Burgess; page B61, B67 by Randy Jones.

PHOTOS

Page B10 (top) Richard Rodamar; pages B10 (top middle) (bottom), B12 (top) James Holland/Stock Boston; B32 (bottom middle), B73, B76, B57-59 by Rhoda Sidney; pages B11 (top) (bottom), B12 (bottom left) (bottom right), B22 courtesy of the Greater New Orleans Tourist and Convention Commission; page B11, B13 courtesy of the Chamber of Commerce of the New Orleans Area; page B32 USDA photo; page B32 (top middle) courtesy of the Rice Council; page B32 (middle) United Fresh Fruit and Vegetable Association; page B32 (bottom) Massachusetts Horticultural Society; page B42 Movie Star News; page B50 (top left) New York Convention and Visitors Bureau; page B50 (top right) (bottom left) by Irene Springer; page B50 (bottom right) by Ken Karp; page B76 (top right) United Nations photo; page B66 New York Convention and Visitors Bureau.

REALIA

Pages B6, B10, B15, B17, B18, B22, B28, B43 (top, bottom), B44 (middle, bottom), B46 (bottom), B51, B56, B62 (top), B78 (bottom) by Roberto de Vicq; pages B42, B63, B66, B73, B76, B78 (top), B79, B80 by Anna Veltfort.

REVIEWERS AND CONSULTANTS

Regents/Prentice Hall would like to thank the following long-time users of *Spectrum*, whose insights and suggestions have helped to shape the content and format of the new edition: Motofumi Aramaki, *Sony Language Laboratory*, Tokyo, Japan; *Associacão Cultural Brasil-Estados Unidos (ACBEU)*, Salvador-Bahia, Brazil; *AUA Language Center*, Bangkok, Thailand, Thomas J. Kral and faculty; Pedro I. Cohen, Professor Emeritus of English, Linguistics, and Education, *Universidad de Panamá*; *ELSI Taiwan Language Schools*, Taipei, Taiwan, Kenneth Hou and faculty; James Hale, *Sundai ELS*, Tokyo, Japan; *Impact*, Santiago, Chile; *Instituto Brasil-Estados Unidos (IBEU)*, Rio de Janeiro, Brazil; *Instituto Brasil-Estados Unidos No Ceará (IBEU-CE)*, Fortaleza, Brazil; *Instituto Chileno Norteamericano de Cultura*, Santiago, Chile; *Instituto Cultural Argentino Norteamericano (ICANA)*, Buenos Aires, Argentina; Christopher M. Knott, *Chris English Masters Schools*, Kyoto, Japan; *The Language Training and Testing Center*, Taipei, Taiwan, Anthony Y. T. Wu and faculty; *Lutheran Language Institute*, Tokyo, Japan; *Network Cultura, Ensino e Livraria Ltda*, São Paulo, Brazil; *Seven Language and Culture*, São Paulo, Brazil.